Drawing Out the Muses

Find and develop
unlimited creative inspiration
from the everyday world

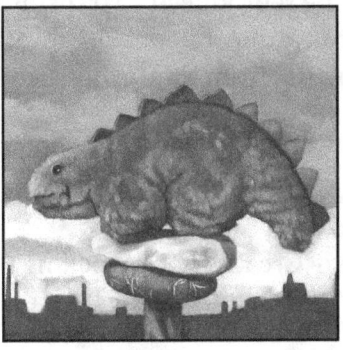

© 2014, Alexandria Levin
Painted Jay Publishing, LLC
www.paintedjay.com

Updated and revised from, and previously published as;
Creatively Unblocking Creative Blocks
Over 300 fun ways to get your visual creative motor going again!

Drawing Out the Muses

Find and develop unlimited creative inspiration from the everyday world

Published by Painted Jay Publishing, LLC
www.paintedjay.com

ISBN: 978-0692300961
Updated and Revised from 'Creatively Unblocking Creative Blocks'
Published in the United States of America in 2014
Printed by CreateSpace

Cover painting: 'Stegosaurus'
© 2008, Alexandria Levin

Interior artwork: © 2004–2008, Alexandria Levin

Acknowledgements

At the very beginning, my gratitude has to go to my fellow artists. They have studied with me in art classes and at art college. We have shown our artwork in exhibitions together, worked on installation projects as a community, painted in various studio buildings as neighbors, and have supported one another in a myriad of ways over the years. In the process, we have learned so much from each other.

As a teacher, I would especially like to thank my very first class of painting students at the Harwood Art Center in Albuquerque, NM. They let me know that I really did have something important to share in teaching art, and encouraged me with continuing in my methods.

Of course, I have the deepest gratitude for the artists who came before me, especially the ones who struggled, who fought, and who broke barriers; both social and creative.

Special thanks go to my boyfriend who taught me how to draw representationally, when both art schools I went to couldn't. Being able to draw exactly what I could see in front of me, eventually allowed me to better depict that which is unseen.

Next, I need to acknowledge this one strange and magnificent afternoon that I spent in the European painting wing of the National Gallery in Washington, DC in June of 2000. While standing transfixed before a Vermeer, the people around me went vague, and the gallery dimmed to near silence. What seemed like a beam of light came down upon me. I was nearly in tears, I was so moved. And then, as I wandered the nearby rooms surrounded by the work of the masters, the paintings gave up their secrets to me. I could suddenly see the layers beneath the surfaces. I then came to clearly understand how each and every one was painted, from the bottom on up. This revelation, this knowing, has been one of the greatest gifts I have ever received.

One cannot truly be an artist without being in profound respect of the natural world, as this is the source of all visual beauty; pattern, color, depth, poetry... Without nature, we are nothing.

Art is truly magical stuff, and yet it is as solid as anything on this earth that you can hold in your hand.

Finally, I really have to give it up for the infinite spirit of creativity, which always comes through for me, even when not much else seems to. These are the muses. They are here for you as well, and simply need to be welcomed in by your actions. Unlimited creativity circulates. Enjoy, learn, explore, have fun, play seriously and welcome the spirit of creativity to stay with you for good.

For Your Information / Disclaimer

For my parents,
Florence and Lawrence,
who never stifled
my creativity as a child,
but always encouraged me
to develop my own imagination.

Contents

Contents

Art
is thought
made tangible.

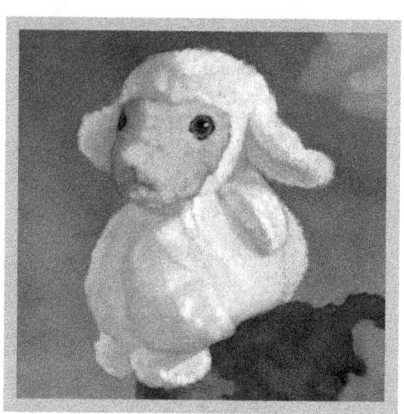

Introduction

Creative blocks are mean and terrible monsters. They keep you from doing one of the things that you love the most, which is creating original, vibrant artwork. They show up unannounced and without an appointment, never giving you advance warning. They lock all the gates and doorways. They board up the windows. They place concrete dividers across the roads. They are rude.

But maybe, in their own special and annoying way, they are trying to tell you something. You might need to follow another path, look at something you already know through new eyes, or think about things differently. This book will show you how.

Creative blocks are sometimes shape shifters. You may be dangling by a frayed thread while hovering over the middle of an abyss of a seemingly endless slump. Maybe you're bored out of your skull with the way you've been making art. Maybe you have this uncontrollable urge to grow and evolve as an artist, but you don't know where or how to start. Or maybe you're humming along just fine, but maybe, just maybe, an idea in this book will spark something that will lead you somewhere else. The next thing you know, your art is taking a wonderful new turn, one that you could never have previously imagined. The possibilities are endless. The artistic impulse for creative expansion is a restless mind, always desiring to improve skills and explore new territories.

The muses are always waiting in the wings. To invite them in, one must take action, even the most simple of actions. This book gives you hundreds of these active starting points, and shows you how to create starting points of your own. Keep yourself open, and the muses will be there for you. Creativity flows.

I have written this book for all visual artists by any definition, at any career level from beginner to accomplished professional, working in any medium, including traditional crafts. It is for any visually-oriented person who is interested in expanding their own creativity. Designers, students, hobbyists, educators, workshop leaders and event planners will find this book considerably useful, as well.

The information, ideas and exercises in this book are designed to help you create better artwork by expanding your creative thinking abilities. You may also find that the exercises herein are good for general problem solving, and can be applied to other areas of your life.

For years, I have been an informal creativity advisor to artist friends (at their request). Awhile back, I wrote and produced a few courses for painting that involved creative methods for teaching technical skills, as well as original approaches for expanding artistic creativity. Designing the curriculum for these courses gave me the impetus to write this book.

This book is divided into two groups of chapters. The first seven chapters are the 'Abouts' chapters. They define and clarify what you need to know about creating artwork, as well as understanding how to best utilize the exercises in the following chapters.

The next twelve chapters are the 'Finding Inspiration' chapters, including an introduction. This is the main body of the book, and these chapters contain most of the explorations and exercises for helping you work through creative blocks. There are varying formats for these eleven chapters, as you will see. They are not all the same.

This is not a book on the psychology or science of creativity. This is an artists' book for getting through creative blocks in a way that is exploratory, productive and fun. It will help you with the process of thinking clearly about art-making. I want to show you that there are countless ways of looking at absolutely anything, with such a wide variety of things to express. Equally innumerable are methods for developing your work. Creativity is truly infinite. The muses are always there for you.

In this one book there are over 300 fun and serious examples, exercises, ideas, explorations, things to do, and ways of seeing and interpreting the world around you, most with multiple variations from which to choose. Every last one is designed to give you something to work on or play with, while helping to spark your own creativity in the process.

When you feel lost, stuck or blocked, use anything in this book that appeals to you to get your artistic motor going. The resulting artwork does not have to look good or be meaningful. Not yet. At this stage, it is all about the process. You may discover many other things along the way that you can apply later to your own finished work, which is an added bonus. But for now, just enjoy yourself while becoming immersed in serious, dedicated play. Take only the advice, and only do the exercises that seem useful or appealing to you.

Begin, explore, create, enjoy, keep learning and continue growing. To break through creative blocks you will need to dedicate some time to doing so. Time commitments sound much worse than they really are when it comes to something that is important to you. Even one hour devoted to your creative endeavors once every week is better than no time at all.

The only discipline you need is to enter the studio, sit at your worktable or curl up with a sketchbook, and simply start doing something. Schedule regular time for this if you can. Make a steady date with your muse. And if you can't, then plan to commit a certain amount of time per week, whenever that time may actually happen to fall in any particular week.

I look for three things in writing; clarity of thought, flow of conversation, and poetry. I apologize in advance for any imperfect grammar, mixed use of tenses and pronouns, or anything else not officially correct. It is more important to me that I express all of these ideas to you with as much lucidity as possible, from one creative person to another, than to be the perfect grammarian. Mistakes will be made. Rules will be broken.

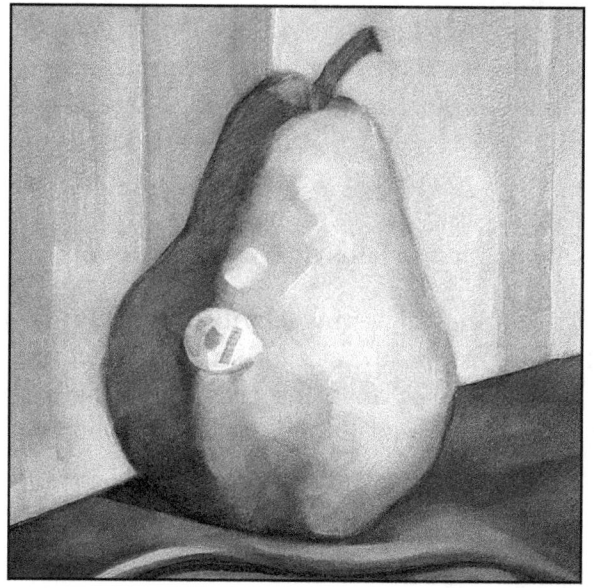

The Nature of Creativity and Inspiration

Creativity is the state of being creative. Being creative means that you have the ability to create. To create is to make something original where it did not exist before, by using one's imagination, and I would also think, by applying some of one's curiosity and intellect as well. To make something original is to make something that was never made quite that exact same way by anyone else until this point in time. Being a creative person means that you do this act of creating quite often, out of habit maybe, and definitely from second nature.

Speaking of nature, creativity is an inherent and defining quality of the spirit of the universe, or however you may call or refer to the divine or that which sets science in motion. Nature is creation in all its glorious achievement. All you need to understand this idea is to simply look around at all the immense variety of everything.

Think of how many categories of birds there are, such as waterfowl, songbirds, game birds, birds of prey and hummingbirds, to name a few. How many species are there within each category, and then again, how many minute variations of each species are there with slight differences in feather or beak or tail? The same goes with trees, sunflowers, fish, tomatoes, roses, dragonflies and dogs. There are over 7,000 types of apples in the world, even though at the grocery store you may only be offered half a dozen to choose from.

Consider all the many kinds of rocks, geologic formations, clouds, bodies of water and fossils there are. Infinity is best approached with snowflakes. Meanwhile, listen to how many songs and other musical compositions can be written from just twelve lonely notes. Twelve basic colors on a wheel and look at how many original paintings have been painted.

To be creative is to look at, or think about, things in many different ways, and then bringing that vision and thought to some kind of form.

Creativity is often seen as only referring to the visual, performing and literary arts, but it is a natural human trait. We are all creative, simply by being human. Non-artists can be just as creative as us stereotypical creative types, only the resulting expression is different. Everything we do as human beings can be informed by creative impulses; cooking, homemaking, gardening, how we dress ourselves, gadgets we invent when the thing we need can't be found at the store; plus the way that roads are designed, how offices are run, and how classes are taught. We can follow the recipes, the sewing patterns and any part of the status quo exactly as they have been given to us, or we can find a more fair, more interesting, more colorful and/or better functioning way for things to be.

We may have been taught to follow all the visual rules, such as; skies only come in blue and all still-lifes must either be flowers in a vase or fruit in a bowl. Follow the recipe exactly, use a particular brand, beds are made this way and tables are set that way.

As a child I did a drawing of a sky with pink clouds. I was scolded by my teacher because clouds were white, not pink. My problem was, however, that I had seen a sunset, and I had seen real pink clouds. From that point on I could have colored all my clouds white to please somebody else, but ever since my skies and clouds have come in all sorts of colors, depending on what the individual drawing or painting wants. Sometimes the sky is blue and the clouds are white. Sometimes they are not. Simple as that.

Stand up for your own sense of variety as an expression of your creativity. If an artistic expression rings true for you, or you want to set the table with the napkins going the other way, then that's what you do.

Expressing creativity is a form of problem solving. It is like a puzzle. There are jillions of pieces and more than one fits the empty space you need to fill. You may have quite a few pieces to choose from.

Open your eyes and you will see that those pieces are everywhere; puzzle pieces sitting on branches outside the window, hiding between books on the shelf, flat on the floor by the kitchen table, hanging from the light cord and floating through the air.

Once you know how to recognize one puzzle piece, you will then begin to spot a few more, and look, there's a whole bunch of them over there. Pretty soon, you will notice hundreds, thousands even, just waiting for you to see if they will fit the space. Then you can pick and choose which one fits best for the puzzle at hand.

All problem-solving, planning, designing, and decision-making is a form of creativity in action. For an artist facing creative blocks, the problem may be, how am I going to express a particular thought? Even scarier is the thought; am I ever again going to have any thoughts to express?

Well, how does one get thoughts? In a way, you think them up. Thinking is done in the conscious mind. Thoughts generally come from the subconscious mind. They come to you when you let them come. You can concentrate on your thinking, but thought, creative thought, comes from the opposite of concentrating. You do this by clearing space, removing the clutter in your mind and seeing what fills in. Thought will then come and fill the empty space. Thought abhors a vacuum. Your job, the task at hand, is to ever-so-lightly be receptive to this thought. Do not judge it. Listen to it, record it, take notes. This is where inspiration comes from.

The word inspiration is related to spire, aspire, respire, and spirit. All are related to the word and meaning of breath, as in that which gives life, or the spark of life from the divine, however one defines the divine. Creativity is the bond between the physical world that our physical selves exist in and the spiritual world. Inspiration is channeling the flow from one realm to the other. Inspiration is tapping into this stream of creativity. If we are each a spark of the divine, then we naturally have this in us.

Inspiration is like sleep. It cannot be forced, it comes when it wants, and only when we allow it to come. For some of us it is easier than for others, but tapping into the flow of creativity is inherent in all of us as human beings. An infinite amount of creative energy is out there waiting to be collected. There is no limit. It is just a matter of making space for it, which is simply a matter of quieting the noise and clearing away the clutter in our minds.

There will come a time when you can tap into your sources of inspiration under almost any circumstance, but it helps to be in a relatively quiet space with no outside distractions. Cleaning out the excess stuff that is making a mess inside your head can easily be done on a short-term basis, long enough to let in a few illuminated sparks to set your imagination aglow. Use basic visualization techniques, where you let yourself clearly see the process inside your mind.

Here are a few suggestions for clearing your mind using visualization:

- A fan outside one ear, blowing all the unnecessary things out the other ear
- A jumbo eraser eliminating that which needs to be gone
- A bunch of colorful balloons carrying the excess stuff into the far reaches of the sky, until you can't see them anymore
- A set of brooms sweeping it all away
- A flock of birds carrying the clutter out through an open window

Come up with your own images to clear your mind, or use any of the above ideas to start. Once the mind-clutter is gone, either pictorial-thought, word-thought or feeling-thought will automatically show up on its own, or it may need a little help. Below are some visualization ideas for tapping into the flow of inspiration:

- Scooping it up from the nearly infinite grains of sand at the beach
- Holding out your cupped hands and letting it fall from the sky
- Collecting it in a cistern on the roof, or through a funnel placed on top of your head
- Tapping into a tree, bucket at the ready
- Dipping a bowl deep into a river, the literal stream of consciousness
- Getting aboard the train of thought, and riding it for all it's worth

I've always defined art as thought made physical, complimented by the use of certain technical skills and a keen sense of aesthetics. That's been my standard definition and I've used it often in my artist statements over the years.

When you exercise your creative muscles, your imagination grows stronger. The more you work at something, the more ideas will come. Of course, there may still be some periodic down time. This is the natural ebb and flow of doing creative work. You take something and run with it. And eventually, you either drop the thing, or you just don't feel like holding it anymore and you put it down. Then you pick up something else.

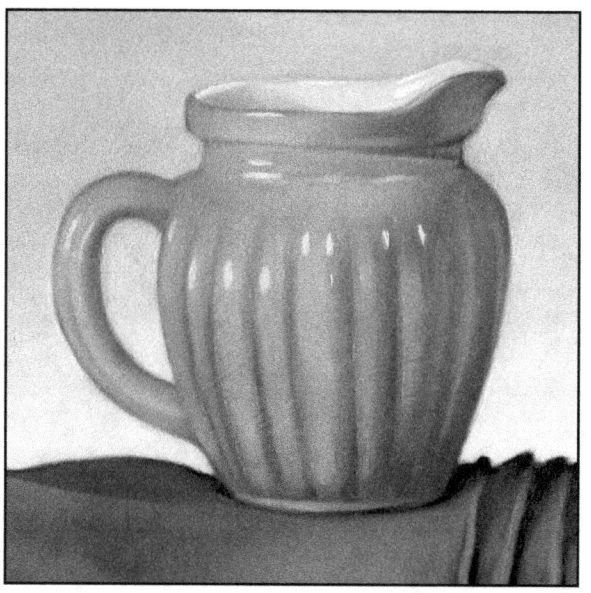

About Serious Play and Not Worrying

Play involves fun, letting go and being in the moment. You are one with your toys, with your materials. Nothing else matters. Nothing else has much of a chance of intruding on your concentration. Serious play is a loose form of concentrating, of directing your mental energy towards what you are playing with. The serious part is your dedication. It is this purposeful getting-lost-in-something where much creativity is born. If you lose track of time and the world goes away, at least for a little while, then you know that the system is working.

Inspiration often comes in momentary sparks during the course of serious play, because you are letting go of the clutter from the outside world. By playing, you are actively clearing your mind, which is very different from being empty-headed. This is the difference between walking forward as you make your way along a path, as opposed to mindlessly walking into a tree. You will discover all kinds of things in serious play about your materials, your methods, your imagination and yourself. When you are deeply involved with what you are doing in a pleasurable way, the ideas will come. Let them all in and see what they have to say. Some will amaze you. Others will amuse you. Some will just be passing through.

Serious play in the visual arts is usually a solo act, and in this book we will treat it that way. If you are in the company of others with whom you are comfortable and have nothing to prove, then that will work too. It is best to not be disturbed; no phone, no doorbell, no television, no interruptions. This time is yours. Sometimes music is helpful, sometimes not. Listen to music that resonates with you personally, and not what somebody else thinks you should be listening to.

You do not have to show any of the pieces you create here to anybody else. Nope. It's all yours, it's all process, and it's probably not finished anyway. You are an artist, not a factory. Part of the quasi-routine of being an artist is that there will be down time. This is normal. The most brilliant minds go blank sometimes. You are in good company.

Your job right now is to play, have fun, explore, and learn. Become interested in, and fascinated by, new materials and approaches to art-making. Get lost in something that may be similar to what you already do, but is different enough to take you out of your usual context in order to shift your thinking, thereby stimulating your natural creativity. Afterwards, you can bring what you have discovered back to enhance and enliven your own regular artwork at a later time, if you so choose.

Worrying about having meaning in your art or making a statement while in serious play will drive you crazy. This will come later. The most meaningful and great artistic statements will come when they are good and ready, and not when they are obliged. Put it all aside for now. Forced meaning is usually trite. Accidental meaning often has surprising depth.

Do not worry about what anybody else is saying or thinking. Do not listen to the chorus, the jury, all those negative voices repeating terrible things. If you feel too isolated when the critics have all gone, call in a committee of creativity angels and muses, and let them keep you company. Close the door on the judgment police. Tell them you are in research and development mode, and it is now time for them to go away.

While you are busy not worrying, remember not to worry about what any of the resulting artwork might look like. That's not important at this time. What is valuable is the process that will someday, sooner or later, lead you to make better artwork that is more fun, interesting, beautiful and/or meaningful for you to create. Your job right now is not to make finished art, but to stimulate the processes that will eventually lead to making much better finished art. But not yet. Later on.

If by accident you paint or sculpt or weave something that is quite stunning on the first go, then that is wonderful. Just make sure that you don't hold it up as a standard for all your other explorations. It may be too much pressure to repeat, and the last thing that the process of serious play needs is pressure.

Using Restrictions and Guidelines for Stimulating Creativity

Once upon a time, I made an exchange with a friend who was teaching in Japan. She had been wanting to own one of my paintings for years and she also wanted me to visit her in Japan. I wanted to go to Japan and I wanted her to have one of my paintings. We decided to trade a two-week trip to Tokyo, everything included except for spending money, in exchange for a painting which I would create upon returning to the U.S.

When discussing details such as size, we made easy agreements. Her only aesthetic requirement for the painting was that it include "at least one fish". She knew my work, and decided that anything else I did was okay by her. This was the most enjoyable commission I have ever agreed to do. I loved that there was this simple parameter; "at least one fish".

There is a big difference between "paint anything" and "paint at least one fish". "Paint anything" can be overwhelming. With a guideline like "at least one fish", I had something to work with. I could ponder... At least one fish, or maybe more fish, what kind of fish, what are they doing, where are they going, are they swimming, and if so, where? Was it the creature fish, the food fish or maybe the sport fish? Fish, wish, swish, dish, disk, asterisk.

All kinds of possibilities arose. There was so much to work with. So many worlds opened up, as you will see, instead of a big overwhelming blank white canvas staring back at me with the words "paint anything" echoing away inside my head.

Go to this page on my website (http://alexalev.com/book-references. html) to see the resulting piece called The Tree of Life. I took images and stories from my friend's and my common travels to New Mexico and Japan (I was living in San Francisco at the time), combined with an interest in the archetypal tree of life, to create the picture that you see.

It might seem that creativity, being sparked by the spirit of the infinite universe, would be at severe odds with such things as restrictions and guidelines. Not so, because the limitations are self-imposed and/or agreed-upon, and they are chosen from a vast array of options. Restrictions, by limiting certain choices, almost by necessity spark other creative choices.

I remember noticing a group of teenage girls in parochial school uniforms; same plaid skirt, maroon sweater and white socks. But each one did something different and interesting with her hair using ribbons, braids, clips, bands and barrettes. They might not have done this if they had more freedom to choose their own dress, and instead sported the same matching ponytail as every other teenage girl from that time.

A guideline is something used to assist you through unfamiliar territory. It is not to tell you exactly where to go, but to keep you moving forward on a path and away from the rattlesnakes lurking in the brush. Restrictions and guidelines are only starting points. They are the places from where you launch brilliant shooting stars. For example:

Consider the color yellow, various linear elements and the number three. Now, apply that to any medium, style or approach to making a piece of art, or maybe even a series of pieces. The variety of interpretations among artists will be stunning. Or try this: Which of the two following points is more stimulating to your creativity?

1. Be creative. C'mon, go ahead.

2. Create something, anything in your chosen medium utilizing the following visual elements; the color yellow, an assortment of lines and the number three.

See? Chances are you immediately saw something, maybe a flash of a picture came to mind, or within a few minutes an idea for a trio of pieces came to you. Even these three simple elements have stimulated creative thought. You saw 'yellow, lines and three' compiled in not quite the same way as anyone else reading this chapter saw them. The notable thing is that you saw something, anything. You are probably still seeing the images right now. And you will keep seeing them, maybe even rearranging them for at least a few minutes, quite possibly longer. You are a visual person. You cannot help this.

The following chapters contain many such examples and exercises. As another example:

1. Do a clay sculpture. Be creative (especially when you are not feeling creative).

2. Do a clay sculpture of a lamp.

Here you have a little direction, a guideline, but no other restrictions. Now what do you do? You work within the confines of the word "lamp", this being the sole restriction. Try doing some free-writing or wordplay (explained in the next chapter) with the word "lamp", or begin by making a list of all the kinds of lamps that you can think of. You can play with aesthetic considerations only, give the chosen lamp personality, or play with the idea or concept of one lamp in particular or lamps in general. Maybe you can make clay letters spelling out "l-a-m-p". But start somewhere, and go:

Table lamp, floor lamp, gooseneck lamp, gas lamp, street lamp, chandelier, a hanging lamp... okay, gooseneck lamp. Goose, geese, fleece, feathers, down, up... a lamp on winter migration, with a scarf around its neck... flying, floating, swimming, honking... a lamp that honks. Clay, yes, but maybe I can add a bicycle horn too.

Some of the results may very well be silly, but they will most likely be creative. Guidelines and/or restrictions are only the starting point. This method is quite the opposite of controlling your creativity. By keeping in mind a few concepts or designated visual elements, your ideas and interpretations become infinite beyond those starting points, and are restrained only by the boundaries of your chosen material.

Having a specific problem to be solved invokes creativity. A problem is a type of puzzle. For example, "How am I going to portray or express anything in this vast universe, when I have everything in this vast universe to choose from?" It's an open problem, simply because it is overwhelming. It's wide open, as wide as the universe. If the issue a hand, instead, was to portray or express something in purples and blues that evokes a sense of grandeur, this will push your creativity by making you think of how these colors can possibly do that.

It's all about there being way too many choices to choose from sometimes, and too many voices telling you too many different things at once. When you break down the choices by giving yourself some guidelines, it becomes not so overwhelming.

As a practical example, let's say you decide to re-decorate your living room. What color are you going to paint the room? How many thousands of colors of wall paint are there? Yikes! Too many! But if you decide to paint the room green, there are now only a few hundred interior paint colors to choose from. It's much easier and you can narrow things down from "green". You can decide if you want a dark, light or a bright green, or a green that leans towards blue or yellow, or maybe even aim for a two-tones-of-green situation. All these clearer choices are there for you, just by deciding to paint the room green instead of any color at all.

Chances are you already focus on something; be it subject matter, meaning or material. These exercises will help push what you already do further, make it better, and may even open up some new avenues for you. By playing, exploring and learning this way, you can bring all kinds of good stuff back to what you usually do. You may even decide to shift your work in another direction.

This is why I find theme shows to be so interesting. Based on a guideline or restriction, these group exhibitions display such a wealth of creativity, with differing viewpoints of the selected theme. They have more personality, are more fun and can be much more thought-provoking than open group exhibitions, at least in my opinion, and only if they are well-curated, of course.

Brainstorming and Free-Writing

Brainstorming and free-writing are two commonly used methods to stimulate creativity. Although both methods use language as a basis, they can be very effective for the visual arts as well. Brainstorming is verbal and list-oriented, and free-writing, of course, is written.

Brainstorming

Brainstorming is a free-association process, usually done in a group of any size. To brainstorm is to banter back and forth between the subconscious and the conscious minds, with all members of the group joining in. It is a quick and spontaneous playing with thoughts and ideas, without judgment, for a specific purpose.

How to brainstorm:

You begin with announcing the subject at hand to all the participants. Brainstorming uses a starting point; a specific problem, an issue, or a single word or phrase. You begin with consciously thinking, and then you let the thoughts follow through. Say absolutely everything that comes to mind, and record all of it the moment it has been said. It is best to write down these thoughts and ideas with pen, pencil or keyboard, so that they can be viewed all at once after the brainstorming session has ended. Write everything down, no matter how silly, absurd, or useless the ideas may seem. You never know when one seemingly absurd thought may be the key to the perfect solution you were hoping to find. There is to be no judgment, and absolutely no editing during the process of brainstorming, not even from yourself. You are finished when the group runs out of ideas.

After the brainstorming session, review everything that has been recorded, and then begin the editing process. You can let your written notes simmer overnight or for a few days, although it is best to go over them sooner than later. When everyone is all brainstormed-out and the spontaneous ideas have run dry, take a break. Upon returning, you can edit the list of ideas when everyone is refreshed and clear-headed.

For visual artists, brainstorming can be useful for generating ideas for commissioned work, when you need to produce work to fit the theme of an exhibition, murals, installations, or anything involving the use of metaphoric or allegorical content. Below are two simple examples of brainstorming.

Problem: Ideas are needed for a mural that will be painted on a wall behind a community garden
Artists: A group of five muralists
Starting words: Community Garden

Begin brainstorming:

Garden, the idea of the garden, what is growing, how about the community itself as growing in a garden, children of all sizes sprouting from the ground as the fruit of the plants, the idea of urban farming, farming up a bargain, what about the design aspect of the mural, maybe rows of things, beets and peas in a row, roses in a grove, a geometric pattern made from all kinds of produce, how about a garden growing up to reach the sky, morning glories and other vines with tendrils wrapped around the heavens, a grape arbor in the stars, day and night and sun and moon, garden plants growing from the rooftops, reaching planets, passing clouds, water sprinkling from the clouds like watering cans...

This group of muralists now has a number of possibilities for the mural. To edit the above, they would read through all of the ideas one at a time and ask for feedback from the group. Some ideas will be of interest, and others will be tossed out or put aside for another project. If there is one favorite idea, then that one can be expanded with brainstorming, as well.

Problem: You need to create three pieces of fiber art on the theme of light.
Artist: One individual artist
Starting exercise: Come up with all meanings of the word light

Begin brainstorming:

"Light, to alight on something, to step lightly, light like a lamp, the sun, reflected light, a degree of or a lack of or minimal weight, light like lite, light in tint like light blue. Woven pictures of the sun, of rays of light, use light colors, all light colors with minimal value contrast, dark pieces with fabric rays of light emanating from the center or edges of the piece, giant crocheted light bulbs, ooh, that's kind of fun, but not very profound, is this supposed to be serious or... light, okay light, then it works, what else, something with shiny reflective fabric and hidden tiny strings of lights, maybe things floating in air that normally shouldn't be able to do so."

From the above brainstorm list there are now a number of potential ideas for this project. Decide which ones you like best, and then work with them. During the editing process you could sketch quick ideas, make diagrams with arrows, and add some more notes. Continue to brainstorm with your chosen ideas. The purpose is to both think consciously and let the thoughts flow, no matter how absurd they may seem at the moment they first arrive.

Free-writing

Free-writing is different from brainstorming in that it is usually a solitary process. It is generally spontaneous, and the writing is done without stopping within a set period of time. Free-writing can be useful for specific purposes, but you can also use this method for coming up with word images for creating new work.

Although free-writing is a process primarily geared towards writers, it can be useful for visual artists as well. Of course we think (visualize) in pictures, but we also think in words. Words are necessary here as a tool, an intermediary between spontaneous thought and visual outcome. As we read in the last chapter, simply by hearing or seeing the words; yellow, line and three, we saw something. Words can stimulate visual images.

And even though free-writing is thought of as a solo effort, a room full of people free-writing all at once could be interesting. Afterward, the individuals can compare notes, and expand on their ideas from there.

How to free-write:

Free-writing is an empty-your-head process done quickly within a limited time frame. You may have a starting word or not, depending on whether you are exploring a specific subject, or just seeing what comes on its own. Consciously empty your head and don't be concerned about meaning. If you need help with this, see the suggestions for cleaning out your mind in the first chapter. Begin with one word and then go.

Start with a solid ten minutes. Go longer if you like. Set a timer or an alarm clock, so that you are not paying attention to the time. It will distract you. You can fill a page in ten minutes if you don't stop. You may end up writing lists, go off an a nice long rant, or simply have some fun with word associations. There are no rules about what you write. The important thing is to keep writing until the designated time is up.

Don't worry about handwriting, spelling or punctuation. It is better to do this with a pen and paper, than on the computer. You can polish it up later with the keyboard and screen, but not just yet. The actual writing will be clearer, faster and more automatic if you do it by hand.

You can write about anything. You can write about writer's block, artist's block, about how miserable you feel, about how untalented you are this particular week, all the things cluttering up your desk, your studio, the weather outside, whatever is pressing at the moment. You can even begin by making a list of what you ate for breakfast this morning. This will get you writing, and once you start, you may be surprised at all the creative thoughts that begin to appear. A completely free free-writing session, with no particular subject matter, may begin like this:

"I am stuck stuck stuck barnacle stuck to a boat afloat in the muck though all that which is stuck river tries to run into the sidewalls water falls lands into a pond that is contained nowhere to go and builds up, see the tire rolling by, falls to its side wobbles around, water pools, the turns to ice, nothing gets by, the buildings alight electrical inside they grow brick by brick until they hit the bottoms of the low slung clouds then stop water sopped up giant rags playing tag tying themselves up in knots like giant things riding on swings going only so far once around the pole on the very tippy top the whole thing falls over on its side glancing at what was once a wild ride water slip-slides back to its source but only of course said the chestnut hobby horse."

That's about five minute's worth. You will see from the list below that quite a few pictorial images can be gleaned from this. These may not be great artistic statements, but then again, your own free-writing exercises might produce some amazing things.

- Barnacle stuck to a boat afloat in the muck
- Water falls lands into a pond that is contained
- See the tire rolling by, falls to its side wobbles around
- The buildings alight electrical inside they grow brick by brick
- Giant rags playing tag tying themselves up in knots
- Giant things riding on swings
- What was once a wild ride water slip-slides
- But only of course said the chestnut hobby horse

The other way to free-write is with a theme or a starting word related to that particular theme. Going back to the individual artist who needs to create three pieces of art on the theme of light, he or she could set the timer for ten minutes and begin writing with the word "light".

"Light, lamplight, starlight, neon bar light, darkness in the park, it's kinda stark, but a dog's gotta bark, streetlight corner, lighter than air, but beware, buyer beware cause it's a light fingered situation, soft and light, like lite margarine, light yellow, light gray, make this stuff go away, put it away for another day, oooh, hmmm, dum de dum hum hummingbird lighter than air goes to the fair, where the neon lights go round and round, spinning like a top that's out on the town, starlight so pretty over the lit-up orange vapor streetlight city, so bright, dimming out the pale moonlight..."

When you drift away from the theme, nudge yourself back. Let go of conscious thought while in the process of free-writing, but catch yourself when you wander too far away. You can see how the above example drifted away and was gently guided back to the word light. Now, see how many more word-images have been created. Some of them may be very useful to the artist, whether as a direct idea, or as a spark for something else.

Word Associations

This is simply playing with rhyming, phonics and speech sounds, as well as with the meaning of words. A lot of my own free-writing gets moved forward by playing with word associations. In essence, this is building a chain or passage of words that relate somehow to the one before it, one word to the next.

A simple word association might go like this:

Red, bed, better, bet, all set, go get all wet, the sun will set red, orange, yellow, funny fellow, kinda mellow...

Here is a double-word association, as an example:

Another word, a butter bird, a herd all-a-blunder, while thunder is heard down under...

The Basic Visual Elements of Art

The following is a list of the basic, essential visual elements of art, along with their definitions. Many of these items are compositional elements. Even though some of them may seem to stand alone at times, they usually intertwine and overlap with each other. These visual elements are listed here for your understanding and clarity, as they will be mentioned often in this book.

Composition

Simply defined, an arrangement of parts making up the whole. With art, this arrangement is composed of any number of visual elements. A good composition has a sense of unity among all the parts, even if some of them may seem disparate from each other.

Color

The use of color in creating artwork involves two major things; color theory and the colors of your materials. It is good to know basic color theory and the color wheel; the primary, secondary and tertiary colors, about value, tints, shades, complimentary colors and so on. I understand color instinctively, not as a scientist, so I will not go deep into color theory at this time. Understanding the principles is all most artists really need, and I do suggest that you familiarize yourself with the color wheel, basic theory and language.

What is important, however, is having familiarity with the colors of your medium, which will initially be limited to what the material manufacturers provide. If you make your own, such as dyeing yarn with your own hand-made dyes, then it will only be limited by the scientific facts of your materials. However, reds in pigments, dyes or earth will not match or behave exactly the same as the reds on the color wheel. The nature of colors in your media is quite variable from standard color theory. It takes time to understand the behavior of your colors. Treat this as a fun exploration. If you knew the exact formula to make that certain shade of teal you desire, you would not discover all the other wonderful blues and greens along the way. Different colors, such as with oil paint, also have the qualities of being transparent, translucent or opaque.

Color mixing in material comes two ways, depending on the medium you work in. Pigments or dyes may be mixable; in paint, ink, glazes or powders. Some materials that are not able to be mixed to create a new color are stained glass, colored pencil, fiber, wood or stone. These can be made into combinations by proximity only.

Contrast

Contrast is found in the degree of difference between where one thing ends and another begins. Contrast can be signified by color, value, texture, handling of material, or actual material. A sharp contrast between edges will draw attention and lead the eye.

Light

Light is that which illuminates, or is a reflection of a source of illumination. Light allows you to see something, besides complete darkness. It is also a value of a color or a shade of gray. A light color either is a hue unto itself, or a tint of a darker hue, or is the result of light falling on something that would seem to be a darker color (to whatever degree) otherwise.

Shadow

A shadow is the result of light being blocked in its path by an object or a figure, or even by the very thing that light falls upon. When a shadow of one thing falls upon something else it is called a cast shadow. Shadows are darker than surrounding areas of the same object, but they are not necessarily dark hues unto themselves. It is a comparative darkness. Often, you can see light reflected in the shadows.

Mass

A mass is a gathering together of related visual elements into a larger whole. In drawing or painting massing usually refers to large groupings of shadow shapes as they fall across disparate objects or separate anatomical features on a figure.

Line

A line is a mark that is much longer than it is wide. A line can be long, short, thick, thin, smooth, rough, broken, dotted, fluid, brushy, vertical, horizontal, diagonal, straight, curved, zig-zag or suggested by edges.

Edge

Edges may be found at or near the end of the picture plane or form, or at or near the end of an object or design element within the picture plane or form. An edge is the visual and/or actual end or side of something.

Balance

Balance can be found when there is an equilibrium; a visually well-distributed weight of all the elements utilized in a piece of art, through the use of color, contrast, line, the size and placement of objects, and so on. Some elements of balance include symmetry, vertical and horizontal lines and their placement, odds and evens, and edges. Symmetry can either be lateral, which means by halves like us, having a left and a right side, or radial, which means radiating from the center like a daisy.

Balance is not exactitude in a composition, as this will create visual stasis. The horizon line should not be dead center, but at the very least, slightly higher or lower than halfway between top and bottom. Very high or low horizon lines can be compelling. Vertically centered is iconic. It can be interesting to place some elements off-center if the main object is vertically centered.

Odds and evens refer to the number of dominant objects or elements utilized in a picture plane. Odd numbers are generally considered better for a balanced composition. There is a challenge that lies in using even numbers in the picture plane (and is therefore worth trying). In three-dimensional work, this might not be as much of an issue. The edges of the picture plane can be a very interesting place. If an element goes off of one side, pay attention to balancing that element somehow in another area of the picture.

Tension

This is when the balance is not easy, but is still balanced. Do not confuse this with a piece of art being off-balance, which will give it the sensation or actuality of falling over. Balanced tension can make for a dynamic composition.

Pattern

Pattern is created by adding design elements, pictorial icons, random marks or geometric shapes located on the surface of, well, anything. If something is patterned, then it is not finished with a flat solid color, with or without slight shading or a fade into another color. Patterns are usually repetitive, but not always.

Repetition

When there is more than two of something, usually a multitude of that something, as part of a whole. Repetition can refer to a regular pattern of some kind, as well as exact or similar copies of elements, items, a group of objects, or a row of something.

Perspective

The view from the viewer, from which position something is portrayed. Perspective can be seen from different angles, side to side, above and below, or directly in front. The vanishing point, used often with perspective, is a spot on the horizon line where all pictorial lines lead to. Multiple perspectives at once means looking at something from a few different viewpoints at the same time (such as with Cubism).

Path

The path is the route that the eye follows when looking at a picture plane or form. There is usually a place where the viewer begins to look at the piece or visually enters a picture, such as a bright color or a face. Angles and triangles are compositional elements used to encourage the eye to travel. There is often a place for the eye to rest, so that the artwork is not thoroughly busy and the vision is confused. Both straight and curved lines can lead the eye on a path.

Triangles

The word triangle used in reference to visual compositions relates to threes, and often makes for strong compositions. There are a few ways for triangles to exist in the picture plane. One is the position of the objects; follow the general outline to make a triangle. Another is to place three similar objects in different areas of the picture, thus making a triangle. The use of color; three different areas using similar shades or hues of orange for example, can also make for a triangle. You are looking for three similar things in number that are not arranged in a line, three spots of color, or a three-sided prominent shape.

Form

Referring to a three-dimensional object such as a sculpture, or something three-dimensional portrayed in two dimensions, such as the human figure. The form of something is also its shape.

Texture

The feel or look of the surface of something such as glossy, matte, rough, smooth, woolly, fuzzy, furry, ridged, prickly and so on.

Material

Paint, pastel, ink, paper, wood, metal, stone, glass, yarn, clay, etc. Not the art medium, but the raw material itself, which is often called the same as the medium, but is another way to think about it.

Size, Space and Volume

How much ground, air or wall does something occupy? Is it big or small, and are these actual measurements or comparative proportion and scale to something else? What is the viewing distance and visual impact of the piece?

Object

An object is anything that can be seen or touched. In art, an object can be the piece of artwork itself, or it can be anything that is represented by the artwork.

Subject

In art, the subject is often the person, creature or item that is the focal point of the piece. It may also be the theme or meaning, which would then be the subject matter of the piece.

Meaning

Meaning is defined as the interpretation of the subject matter of a piece of art.

Abstraction and Creativity

Here is the history of abstract art in a tiny little nutshell. The first rebellion of the modern age was realism, pure realism, by artists such as Millet, who were reacting against historical, religious and romantic subject matter. The important new subject became real life, thus realism. The next group of artists became concerned with aesthetic issues, like the impressionists (although they didn't call themselves by that name) who were interested with the effects of light falling on scenes of everyday life. This was a new way of seeing the world. Then came cubism, looking at objects from many angles at once. All kinds of other -isms came about in the early decades of the 20th century. Abstraction originally evolved from different ways of looking at and interpreting real things; tangible objects, people, places, and creatures.

Then came World War Two. In the aftermath, many artists began looking for a pure art form either in escapism from or rebellion to all the horrors they had recently observed and/or experienced. Pictorial elements were considered useless, hopeless, in reaction to the war. Soon afterward, abstract art became self-referential, art about art. The movement seemed to get stuck for a while after that, both in time and artistic approach. Outside of any larger movement though, there are many individual artists who work abstractly and do excellent work.

Abstraction means to look at something in a different way, not as it actually appears in a representational manner. There might or might not be a picture involved, and any real-life objects may be presented abstractly. Abstract art emphasizes the use of material, color (or lack thereof), composition, and sometimes raw thought or emotion. Abstract art can be an expression of metaphor using purely visual elements.

Abstraction, in all its phases and fresh for its own time, was a very necessary and exciting series of artistic expressions. We can learn great things from both looking at the work and creating some ourselves. Abstract elements and approaches combined with realism can make for some very exciting work if done well. And it all begins with serious play.

Creating art by employing abstract methods can be very liberating, no matter the creative block you are trying to get through. Working abstractly can open up the imagination, even for dedicated realists, by breaking the artistic process down into the visual elements (see the previous chapter) with the possible exceptions of object, subject and meaning. By playing intently with the materials and the visual elements you will naturally loosen up. It could be pure play, expressing something beyond the visually tangible, like an emotion, or it can simply be diving deeply into aesthetics. It will most likely be a very exploratory process, pushing the materials further than you ever have before. You will learn many things along the way that you can apply to your finished work later on concerning color, composition and the handling of your materials. This is how you develop new ways of applying paint or knotting threads or carving wood.

Absolutely do not be concerned with making bad art when any of these exercises are here to simply get you on a path of exploration. There is a different standard between playing artistically, even serious play, and creating finished work and calling it art.

By going abstract, especially if you do pictorial work, by stepping outside of your habitual self, you will learn much. By looking at things from a totally new angle, the view can be amazing and quite liberating. If you already do abstract work but feel stuck, then take a different approach. If you relate to being a realist, don't worry about the label. You are not wearing a tag, and if you are, it simply says "artist". Most of the great ones in history experimented and explored. It's called curiosity. And curiosity is a sign of intelligence. None of the masters did the same thing over and over and over again.

Take different ways of looking at things by removing expectations, both yours and others'. You are free to explore and play. If there is a roadblock in your creativity, know that there are countless other roads to take where the path is clear.

Translating from One Medium to Another

There is no set formula, scientific or mathematical equation for the translation of ideas from one medium to another. You will have to use your own imagination and personal knowledge of your medium for doing this. However, there are many things you can do in shifting ideas from one art form to something else. The flexibility involved in doing this can open up countless new ideas for you.

The exercises and explorations in the following chapters may be done exactly as recommended in the materials mentioned as examples, or they can be translated to any other medium. There are no limits, except those imposed by the physical nature of any given material.

Many of the exercises will be written for two-dimensional art, but there are at least a few examples for three-dimensional work in each chapter. Work with your regular medium or play with a new one. Either way, you will learn new things. Artists accustomed to working in two-dimensions can try some of the exercises in a three-dimensional medium such as clay or fiber, and vice-versa. You will find this to be an excellent way to step outside of yourself, since you would probably have few preconceived expectations, if any at all. It is much easier to take a new path when there is no pressure to produce good work every time. Sometimes it is only that constant pressure to achieve which is the greatest creative block of all.

If you are exploring a new medium, but don't wish to seriously invest in it just yet, try working with children's art supplies. Look in regular art supply stores, hobby stores, toy stores or the toy department of discount stores. Student-quality paints are fine for some of these exercises, although I do not recommend them for actually learning about the medium of paint itself. For using color in the medium of clay without going through the process of glazing, you can work with children's modeling clay which comes in colors, or possibly even make it yourself from scratch.

To translate an exercise from one medium to another is to simply shift your thinking just a tiny bit. Take the parameters of the example that is given, and either use them exactly as they are or apply them to your medium. You can do some brainstorming or free-writing pertaining to the subject. List all the definitions you can think of that relate to the idea or item, go beyond my explanations and apply. The following is an example of how to do this.

If I say "paint a circle", what will you do? What can you do? Well, you can do lots of things.

First, let's define what a circle is. You can look the word up in the dictionary, or do a little brainstorming on your own. How do you define what makes a circle? Maybe it's a disk, a ring, a ball, a globe, a sphere, an orb, or a spiral with an enclosing outer ring. Expand that circle to a tube, a cylinder, or a cone. What about other meanings of the word circle besides the defining shape of something, such as a circle of friends? The different meanings can go much further. However, for this example, let's work with variations on the shape circle.

Paint a circle, draw a circle, cut a circle from glass, knit a circle. Three-dimensional mediums get the benefit of both disks and balls being circles. Well okay, technically circles are two-dimensional creatures, but we are going to push the interpretation of the word. After all, this is infinite creativity speaking.

So, when I say "paint a circle", you can do any of the following things to start, and then go further when your mind is sparked. These are only a few examples in a few assorted mediums to get you thinking in the translation process. Chances are that simply by reading through the ideas that are listed, you will be inspired to think of even more things that you can do with circles.

Paint a circle.

Painting and drawing:

An outline ring; solid, dashed or dotted. A series of concentric rings and a dot in the middle like a bullseye. A solid flat disk in one color. A disk with a pattern of stripes, polka dots, tiny flowers or random splotches. Edge-to-edge painted on a circular canvas or drawn on a cut-out circle of paper. Thin paint, thick paint, scratchy or smooth drawing (or any other surface treatment) on any circle. A two-dimensional circle perfectly shaded to give the illusion of a three-dimensional ball.

Knitting and crocheting:

An outline ring, a solid disk, a chain of rings or disks linked together. A ball, a globe made of smaller balls, a chain of balls. Granny circles. Different stitches, colors and types of yarns, maybe with embellishments such as round beads or sequins. A fuzzy pompom.

Stained-glass:

A circle of glass in one piece. A number of round pieces or medallions soldered into a disk. A number of jagged, broken pieces soldered into a disk. A number of stained-glass pieces soldered into a globe. Stained-glass pieces used as a mosaic set into a disk. One consistent color, two colors, multi-colored.

Clay:

A ring, a solid disk, a ball (with a tiny air hole, of course). Mosaic tile pieces set into a disk. A series of disks or balls attached in a larger circle or ball. Stacked disks. Disks or balls with patterns carved into them.

Wood carving:

A ring, a solid disk, a ball. Disks or balls with patterns carved into them. A ball with a carving hollowed out into one side.

Photography:

Pictures of all kinds of circles and circular things. Color or black and white. Digitally manipulated. Photographs printed on paper cut into circles.

Other variables to any medium:

Personal choice and interpretation. Material handling, color, pattern, repetition, embellishment, meaning.

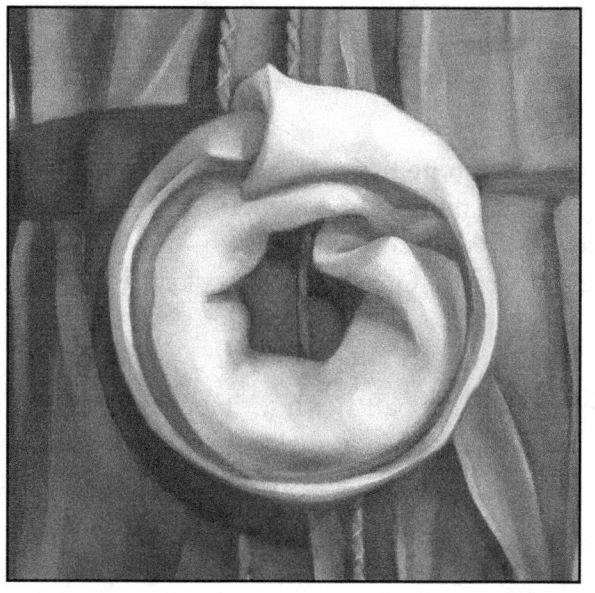

Introduction to Finding Inspiration

The following eleven chapters are divided into categories of things, chosen as examples, where you can find inspiration for creating visual art. The basic premise is that anything; a bumblebee, a leaf, a kitchen sponge or the simple act of loafing on the sofa can be inspirational. By obsessive inventiveness, I show you how to expand ways of looking at, and thinking about, various things, thereby giving you plenty of ideas for developing your own creativity. In these chapters there are hundreds of ideas, exercises, examples, suggestions, different ways of looking at and interpreting things, and so on. Some of the chapters are heavy on the exercises, whereas others discuss visual philosophy.

There are no pictorial examples included in this book that are directly related to the exercises, mainly because I did not want to influence anybody visually. The idea is for you to become proficient at seeing your own pictures in your own mind. You want to find your personal artistic voice that is not affected by what I have seen inside my head while writing these exercises. What I see when imagining five bees bumbling around inside of a furry blue baseball cap will be different than what you see. If you can visualize things for yourself, you are way ahead of the game.

All of the exercises and suggestions herein are for anyone to use in any way they choose for unblocking creative blocks. You certainly do not have to do them all. Only work with the ideas that appeal to you. You can take my suggestions and let them evolve into your own concepts, infused with your own personal vision. Use my examples exactly as written if you are seriously blocked. Simply by involving yourself in a creative activity, your own imagination will start to flow. Sometimes just by reading through a few chapters, ideas will come to you. Or if you want, you can do every last one of the exercises, and in order if you choose. This will certainly keep you busy for a very long time. This is all about being inspired and sparking your creativity. You may need to not think for awhile, but just keep yourself busy with doing stuff without thinking, in which case follow any of the instructions exactly as written.

You will see that there are more detailed directions and guidelines earlier in this set of chapters. This is so you can get an idea of what I mean by such restrictions. In the later chapters you can take any of my suggestions and then add your own guidelines, such as blue, four and triangular. If I don't give a restriction, then the meaning is open. Some of these ideas involve more thinking, some less so.

Some of the exercises are very simple and others are more difficult, but even this all depends on how each individual artist thinks and functions. Some ideas are more explicit in what to do, while others hint at what can be done. Choose your own level of complexity.

You are welcome to shift any guidelines that are given, and change whatever you wish to fit your own desires. For example, maybe your bee abstract will be 75% yellows and purples, instead of 90% yellows and browns. You can do this process with anything, not just bees. Imagine transposing anything about bees into dragonflies or swans or Gila monsters, for example.

When I give a percentage as a guideline, use it as an estimate. Fifty percent green means something is to be half green. Ninety percent green means almost completely green. You do not need to measure every square inch on your project to see if you really kept it to 90% green. If you are not mathematically inclined, then be visual about it. Look at ten inches on a cheap plastic 12-inch ruler. Mark, or cut off, the last two inches if you need to. Then use each inch as a measure for 10%. Three inches = 30%. The remaining seven inches = 70%. Impress upon your mind the visual relationship between the two and apply that to your piece. There you go.

If I say green, then choose any one hue of green that you like. If I say greens, then you can use them all, or maybe you might decide to limit yourself to forest green, apple green and olive green. That's up to you. The use of plurals means to use more than one of that thing.

The term semi-abstract means something that is recognizable, but not in its natural representational form. It means something that is stylized, partially obscured or changed in some way, but you still know what that original item is.

When I say to design something, I mean to draw, create a maquette, put together a sample, or take some notes and sketch them out on paper. This is a process of beginning to bring thought into the physical world, but not necessarily bringing the whole idea to its final completion. A person can design a dress by creating a wonderful full-color drawing on paper, complete with notes and attached fabric swatches, but this is different from actually sewing and finishing the same dress. Designing, composing; these are the first steps in the process of actually creating something.

The idea here is to realize that you are surrounded by stuff, every last little piece of which can be a great source of visual inspiration to you. If anything, these chapters demonstrate that following chains of thought and wandering through them, can lead to interesting places for an artist to be.

Follow chains of thought on paper through sketches, notes, free-writing and brainstorming, and by dissecting what you see into its various parts and raw visual elements. Eventually, you will be able to dissect most things through your thought processes alone. Take all the loose parts; gather them, discard some, and freely rearrange them as you will. Then rearrange them again in a different way.

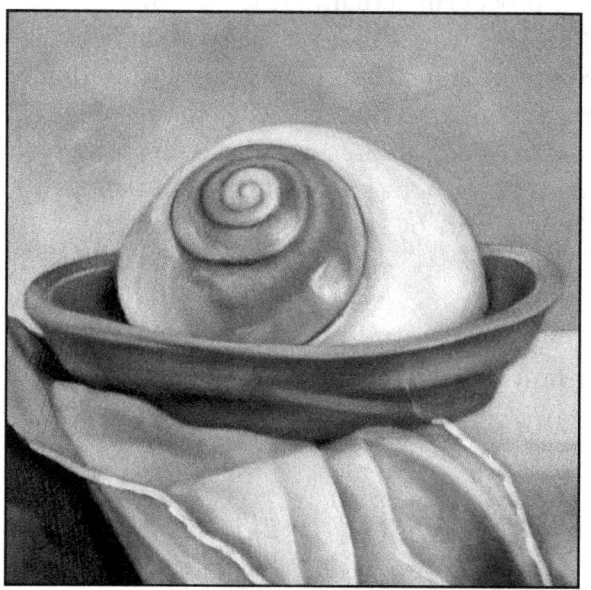

Finding Inspiration in Nature

Bees

As an example of dissecting some of what there is about bees, as the result of a one-person brainstorming session:

Bee elements – Stripes, fuzzy, wings, the hive, honeycomb, honey, flowers, the swarm
Bee concepts – Buzz, sting, dangerous, sweet, workers, drones, queens, pollination

As examples of seeing what both my conscious and subconscious minds might have to say about bees:

Bee brainstorm and word association

Bees, bees knees, bees on the breeze with a sneeze, busily buzzing, fuzzy buzzers, striped in yellow and black fuzzy little jackets, flower to flower by the hour. Buzz, buzz saw, to bee or not to bee. Busy as a bee. Honeybee, bumble bee, fumble bee, bumbling bee. Do bees and don't bees.

Bee free-write

Bees, bumble on a brush in a rush buzz zoom who goes there they all go in a flow well hello bees on the bus what a rush busy buzz honey hive such jive oh no so much stuff honey fluff er where what who why the bees do fly as they are going by in this lower part of the sky...

To do:

1. Do a brainstorm about bees.

2. Do a free-write about bees.

3. Do a word association about bees.

To ask yourself and to do:

1. What images can you see from my two writing samples?

2. What images have you come up with from your own writing?

3. What pictures do you now see by reading the words you have written?

Try depicting what you are seeing from either your word images or mine. Make anything that you want in any medium, in any format, and without restrictions.

All of the following ideas and exercises are rooted in some of the words from the above examples. By exploring what bees are about, you can then take each individual element and concept, and push the ideas a little further, either directly or indirectly. Take ideas, dissect them into their parts, and then expand on those parts. With free-writing and brainstorming, you can add and combine more ideas that are silly, serious, symbolic or pretty much anything else you decide.

Even though some of the subject matter is serious, if you are truly blocked, treat all of this as play. Have fun. Again, you may follow any of the exercises exactly as written, or you may combine, delete, add, or edit ideas as you choose. You can also mix anything I have written here with something else that is truly your own, if you like.

The buzz

Turn the sound into a visual art form, in any medium, in any format, and without restrictions. What does the sound of the buzz look like? What does the vibration of "buzz" feel like, and therefore, what does that feeling look like? Invent a buzzing machine. Draw it or construct it. Give it stripes.

The honeycomb

What can you do with the honeycomb pattern? Use the honeycomb design as a linear 2D or 3D graphic element.

Paint, draw, sculpt or make an abstracted honeycomb, using lines and flat areas based on the honeycomb pattern. Brainstorm or free-write your way to a really cool title for the piece.

The hive

Think of the hive as architecture. What other uses of the hive could there be? Would these hive-themed structures be for bees or other creatures, or even for people to use? Depict or construct your hive-inspired structure. A few ideas: The hive as doll house, parking garage, restaurant, beach cabana and/or artist studio.

Imagine the beehive as designed by famous, distinct and/or historic architects. Design an interpretation.

Colors

Do a semi-abstracted piece using mostly yellow and black to portray the essence of bees in any medium. Make sure that at least 90% of your color use is any shade or type of yellow and black (including very dark gray). The other 10% of the color scheme is up to you. For example, the color usage may be 50% of a variety of yellows, 25% pure black, 15% very dark gray, 5% green and 5% orange. Use at least a few kinds of linear elements and include all or part of three semi-abstracted bees. Now, here's your "yellow, line and three" from the guidelines chapter, with the further constraint of the subject being bees.

Fictional and fantasy bees

What is it about bees that inspires this sort of thing instead of, for example, wasps or flies? Why do ducks get the same treatment, as opposed to seagulls? It's something to ponder. Meanwhile, empty your head of make-believe bees by free-writing, brainstorming or doing a word association exercise. Some examples are:

- Imaginative bees: Duck-billed bees, green and purple-striped bees, bees with other kinds of wings, cartoon bees, bees with television antennae, and world-famous bees.

- The queen bee: Imagine her as a real queen; as royalty, in drag, or as a playing card.

- And speaking of drag: Other creatures, objects and people dressed up as bees.

- Monsters: Scary monster bees, giant bees, swarms of bees as hypodermic needles.

- Busy: Bees doing things besides what bees normally do, such as washing dishes, playing the drums or working in an office.

- Pollinators: Pollinating mailboxes, streetlights, abandoned shoes. I've always thought of buses and bus stops as bees and flowers.

Take one or more of these ideas for fictional and fantasy bees and make them into a portrait or an allegorical scene in any medium.

Contemplative stuff about bees

All of the below can be subject matter for art.

- Serious stuff: The ecological value of bees to crops, the livelihoods of beekeepers, species endangerment

- Scientific stuff: The different types such as honeybees and bumble bees, the swarm, beeswax

- Honey: The nutritional and healing value of honey, the sweetness of honey, turning pollen into honey

- Bee sting: About the sting, allergies, effects on the stinger and the stung

- Political and sociological interpretations in human terms: Workers, the queens, swarms, hordes

Do a serious work, or series of works, about any of the above subjects or issues, or anything else about bees that makes you think. Involve a true statement, a question and an opinion about the bee subject you have chosen. For example: Honey is made by bees. Is it good for me? Well, I think so, but probably in moderation. That was a very simple example. Yours may be as complex and/or as deep as you choose.

Leaves

Leaf elements – Leaf texture, shapes, patterns, clusters, edges, needles, flat, broad, slender, stems, green
Leaf concepts – Shade, photosynthesis, buds, food, foliage, future mulch
Types – Leaves of trees, flowers, vines, shrubs

Leaves as signifiers of time

The leaves are leaving, as they do in the fall, blow away, every day. Blowing like a leaf, change of seasons, passage of time. Brown, drop, crinkle, crust, turn to dust, blow away. Leaves chasing circle in the wind.

Do your own brainstorming, free-writing and/or word association session to begin. Also include the nature of leaves as they cycle through winter, spring, summer and fall.

Do a piece, or a series of pieces, on the theme of the passage of time with leaves as the signifier or the main subject. Make anything that you want in any medium, in any format, and without restrictions except for the theme.

Colors

Spring – Tightly wound pale green, yellow buds
Summer – All shades and types of green; forest green (it's not the bark that everybody is barking about, but the color of the leaves), silver-green, yellow-green, olive green, sage green, willow green, and the deep dark red of red-leafed trees
Fall – All the colors and multi-colors of fall, for which leaves are most famous

Collect a nice assortment of leaves. Try to match the colors of the leaves exactly. This exercise is best for paints, inks, or any pigment or dye-based medium that can be mixed to create completely new colors. For other mediums, you can try matching by proximity.

Symbolism

Consider the Maple Leaf. Imagine if each country, or state, had a leaf flag like Canada. Design flags for any number of countries, states, provinces, counties, cities, towns or villages anywhere in the world, using leaves as the main design element. Think about which colors, graphic elements, and leaves you would assign to represent the places you have chosen.

Shapes and patterns

Collect a nice assortment of leaves as inspiration. Leaves offer up a wealth of two-dimensional shapes and designs. Another possibility is to overlap the leaves to make new shapes (sometimes all you need is a good, interesting shape).

Leaves can be used in printmaking. Make leaf prints. Use a brayer to roll ink on a leaf, and then transfer the inky leaf to a piece of paper and apply pressure. Leaf prints can also be combined with other kinds of printing, rubberstamping, or paper crafts.

Leaves make a wonderful motif for crafts, both functional and purely aesthetic. Use the leaves in a vine, as the central figure, as a whisper of a background, or any other way that you choose.

Abstraction

Do an abstract piece that barely hints of actual leaves, but have it most definitely feel leafy. Have no more than 20% of the picture or structure be recognizable as leaves. Choose three analogous colors from the twelve-section color wheel. Make sure that 90% of your color usage is from those three colors (and slight variations on those three colors), and 10% from any color that is complimentary to any one of those three. For example: 90% orange, red-orange, red and 10% blue-green. Another example would be 90% yellow-green, yellow, yellow-orange and 10% red-violet.

3D possibilities for leaves

Create an installation piece made from piles of fallen autumn leaves. Think about either of the two following questions when designing your installation:

1. What is this urge we have to jump in and kick up leaves?

2. How strange is it that leaves are gathered up and put in garbage bags for trash collection in the fall?

Using leaves that are needles, sew things together, even other leaves. Use the needles in other ways that involve sticking or suturing.

Make a ball of leaves, a wreath, or even a whole outfit that can be worn by somebody or something.

Meaning

Think about the meanings of fig leaves, grape leaves, holly and the olive branch (which includes the leaves). What would be the meanings for other leaves such as oak, cottonwood, or banana? Look at the leaves that live near you. Come up with well-thought-out meanings for each of them. With those meanings, create artwork about your ideas, including images of those particular leaves, or even the actual leaves themselves.

Food and science

Botany and nutrition provide even more leaf themes for artwork. Use the ideas below or explore anything else about leaves that you might like to express with your art. If you are unsure how to do this, combine the intellectual ideas here with visual ideas taken from any other exercise in this book. Use what appeals to you. Remember that something can be serious and fun at the same time, or if seriously serious, it can still be visually beautiful. Play, explore and see what comes to you.

1. Food: For bugs and leaf-eating animals. Leaves are also food for us; lettuce, kale, collard greens, spinach and endive, to name a few.

2. Scientific: The photosynthesis process, pigment, the weather's effect on the color of leaves, classifications of leaves.

The Beach

Beach elements – Horizon line, ocean, sea spray, foam, sand, beach grass, bubble holes, bird tracks, seabirds, fish
Beach concepts – Sound, color, the power and rhythm of the waves, tides and moon, ancient seas and fossils, salt, infinity
Found objects – Driftwood, seaweed, shells, pebbles, stones, sand dollars, starfish

For this section about the beach, I am going to stick with nature. Human activity such as fishing and the typical summer beach stuff can be added, if you like. Do your own brainstorming, free-writing and/or word association session to include these other beach-related subjects, and apply them to any of the ideas and exercises below.

Landscape

Do a representational landscape, but from an angle that you have never seen a beach landscape done before. That angle may actually be a difference in visual perspective, or it may be a variation on typical beach themes.

Do an abstract landscape based on the actual beach. Include many of the visual elements that you see, such as the shapes of broad areas, patterns, line and edges. Do one with a muted palette based on a few of the main colors of the beach (sand, water, sky, etc.). Do a second piece with the same, or a similar, composition, but using as many brilliant and non-beach colors as you like.

Installation

The beach is a great place for creating artwork using location and found materials. Sand castles are an example of this, but the ideas can go much further. By using only things found on the beach, you will not be contributing to the litter problem. You can make flat-in-the-sand pieces, sculptural work or installations. The work can be big or small or anything in-between. You can create a series of pieces, or make a trail leading somewhere (or nowhere). This can be either a solo or collaborative process.

Design – Using what you find on the beach, make flat-in-the-sand or sculptural designs based on pure aesthetics. Place some objects and construct other ones. Weave beach grass and seaweed.

Meaning – Use shell fragments to create the image of a shell, or driftwood and seaweed to create a tree. Make something to express anything about the beach experience; whether it is fun or serious. Use found trash to say something about garbage. Do not add any trash of your own.

Anti-meaning – Create a piece that looks like it has deep meaning, but which doesn't have any meaning at all. Again, use only found objects. Think about how wonderfully puzzling the final piece can be to onlookers. Spell out a made-up title in the sand using shells or other items. Advertise the piece with sand-signs and arrows, up and down the beach. Document the whole process.

Visual interpretations

Transpose the sound, color, power and rhythm of the ocean as it laps or crashes to shore.

Use ribbons, wires, string and other fibers to visually describe the sound of the ocean, either in a fiber piece, a sculpture, or a room-sized installation. Work with your choice of a limited range of colors.

For 2D artists (turn us sideways, we disappear), do a piece similar to the above using line instead of the ribbons, wires, string and other fibers.

Working with the colors of ocean waves, create a piece that does not actually depict waves, but feels like waves.

Create or depict a powerful wave-making machine. Make it appear rusty and salt-bitten, but tough nonetheless. Another option is to make or portray a wave-making monster that is responsible for the workings of the shoreline.

Think about the rhythmic pattern of the waves. Do a piece that is visually based on the same pattern.

Fantasies, dreams, mythologies

Create a piece or a series about imaginary underwater worlds. If you have underwater dreams, use these as a basis for your artwork. What does it feel like to live there? Who else lives there? What do the cities and villages look like? Where is the light source coming from?

Paint or draw a fantasy underwater seascape. Work with a limited color scheme of your choice. Include at least two forms of plant life, at least one fish and a vertical line somewhere off in the distance.

Portray a series of imaginary well-loved and/or notorious undersea creatures. Base your subjects on mythology (ex: mermaids) and reality (ex: fish), but invent new creatures that haven't existed before.

Think about the ideas and meanings of such beach things as infinity, ancient sea fossils, the moon and the pull of the tides. Create an artwork or a series of pieces using any of these concepts as the theme. Involve some scientific fact, along with your own personal mythology.

Seashells

Using at least 50% found shells and fragments, create an imaginary creature that lives inside of a seashell.

Paint or draw a representational still-life of a seashell. Use one shell. Then do the same using a minimum of three odd-number of shells. Do another still-life using a minimum of two even-number of shells. Make the compositions interesting. Portray shells in a way you have never seen shells portrayed before. Pay attention to how the shells are placed and to what is happening in the background.

Create a piece involving the mathematical formula of a shell's design. This can be a semi-abstract two or three-dimensional artwork based on a seashell's geometry. Work with a palette of only the colors found on that particular shell, unless limited by your medium (such as wood or metal). Add a few visual hints of the shell in your piece.

Consider the following thoughts about shells as inspiration:

- Come out of your shell
- Listen to a shell and hear the roar of the ocean, look into a shell and what do you see? (Don't get sand in your eye.)
- Pearls
- Shell's bells
- The shell as shelter

More beach-inspired ideas

Here are more ideas that you can use as a basis for artistic creativity. Work with any of these ideas and concepts in creating art. You may also combine anything from below with another exercise in any chapter.

- Sand: Rocks and shells becoming sand, colors of sand, wet and dry, sand as a material
- Seabirds: Motion, swoop and call, bird tracks and other footprints, evidence
- Waves: Salt, sea spray, glimmers of rainbow in the crashing wave mist
- Sea creatures who come near shore: Sharks, crabs, fish, seals
- Color, pattern, texture, line: Shells, stone, driftwood, seaweed
- Material and design: Starfish, sand dollars, shells, driftwood, beach pebbles and rocks
- Meaning: The star in starfish, the dollars in sand dollars
- Science: The push and pull and churn near the shore, ancient seas, geologic history found in fossils, fossils as design elements and the idea of fossils, the whole body of a sea creature as an art form

The Sky

Sky elements – Rainbow, aurora borealis, vapor trails, weather, blue
Weather elements – Lightning, rain, snow, sleet, hail, fog, tornado, clouds, wind
Time of day – Day, night, dawn, dusk, sunset
The heavens – Sun, stars, planets, moon, constellations as seen from earth
Miscellaneous sky concepts – Flying things such as birds, kites and airplanes, falling objects, looking up, the horizon line, the big sky, the skyline, air pollution, skyscrapers, skydivers

Sky free-write and word association

The sky in your eye heaves a sigh, the clouds they drift south on the breath from your mouth, heave a sigh. It's a parade of vapors, weather on the march and loosely scheduled. A changing cabaret, a colossal display of barometric claims and dank humidity. A rainbow reached around clouds turned upside down, pull the sky close to the ground, they're all on stage dancing, with an aurora borealis curtain and lightning spotlights prancing.

Do a brainstorming, free-writing and/or word association session starting with any of the sky elements listed above.

What images do you see in your own writing? What can you create from what you see now?

I had some earlier notes about how observing the sky tells us the immediate weather, the time of day, and the time of year. If you have enough sky to observe, you can even tell a bit of the weather forecast. So, I was thinking about weather, and such things, when I began my short free-write above. That evolved into creating the following set of exercises.

Diorama

The shoebox diorama is the predecessor to art installations, and may also be seen as a form of stage design.

Create a diorama featuring the elements of weather. Use anything for the box, or build your own box. Include at least three different phases of weather, and have a bit of story involved if possible. Use at least three different types of art materials, for example; paint, yarn and beads, and as another example; glass, metal and paper. Consider your diorama as a maquette for a larger installation or a professional stage set. Have fun with it and make it interesting for yourself.

Dancing

Portray an element of weather as dancing. Include another type of weather in the background doing something else.

Five sky things at once

Choose one thing from each of the five lists at the top of this section (ex: rainbow, sleet, dawn, moon, skyscrapers). Make another diorama, a sculpture or a pictorial piece including all five of these elements. Have them relate to one another in some way.

Color

Do a realist or semi-representational painting of the sky. Duplicate the colors you see in the sky as closely as possible. A few hints: The daytime sky will fade in color near the horizon. The sky is not a solid blue, but includes a bit of yellowish warmth closer to the horizon. Clouds possess an infinitude of colors, shadows and reflections. Spend some time really looking at clouds.

Do the same for a sunset. Sunsets are fleeting, so you will have to work fast.

Paint three more skies, including some clouds, but not using blue, white or gray. Try three very different sets of colors for your sky and clouds. Have there be a horizon line, a simple landscape on the bottom eighth of your composition, so that the sky will be grounded. Choose your colors for purely aesthetic reasons, for example, because you've always liked how certain hues of purples, oranges and yellows look together.

Paint three more skies with the one-eighth landscape at the bottom. Now choose your colors because of the meaning you want to portray. Choose any three emotions or situations, one for each painting. For example, you may want to portray a solitary sadness, the pure joy of an acrobatic circus, and a dusty year of drought.

Another set of three might be; springtime, nervousness and sleep. Think about how the colors that you chose for the sky and clouds emotionally affect the scene.

The big question

Where does the air end and the sky begin? How far up would that be and from which perspective would it be noticed? Think about these things and also the notion of the big sky. What makes a sky big? Why is it bigger in the west than in the east (of the US anyway)? Is it the altitude? What about the narrow sky as glimpsed between canyons of buildings. Do skyscrapers really scrape? Does it hurt? What makes the skyline a silhouette?

Look at the shape of the sky as seen between buildings and geologic forms. Make a piece of art based on one or more of these "negative" shapes. Then work with the one big shape made by the skyline silhouette.

Do a small painting, drawing, print or other 2D artwork. Have the size of the piece be no bigger than 12"x16". The smaller, the better. Express a big, vast, endless sky in the picture plane.

Do another small piece with the proportions of the canvas, panel or paper being very rectangular, at least twice as wide as tall, for example: 8"x16".

Then do a third piece with the same proportions, only vertical.

Do a fourth piece in a perfect square, 14" or smaller. See how the different proportions affect the sense of the big sky. Does working small limit that sense, or is the size limitation irrelevant to the picture?

Think about the issue of where the air ends and the sky begins. Do a free-writing or brainstorming session on the subject. See what word-images or ideas may be culled from your writing. Create a piece of artwork based on the words and/or ideas that come to you.

Another big question

How does one create a sculpture, or other 3D piece of art portraying the sky? The atmosphere, sky, and air can be portrayed using any 2D medium that focuses more on mass than line. Lines in the sky would be power lines, vapor trails, sun rays through clouds and not much else. Sky is a mass, broken up by clouds, but it is mostly mass. Some clouds have line, especially if they are back-lit. But still, how can the sky be portrayed in three-dimensions?

I did a brainstorm/free-write sort of thing and came up with this:

The sky is a sort of solid thing, hear it sing in the ringing of the wind. It is full of microscopic particles, a congregation of tiny solids. As a whole, a permeable mass, not waterproof, a gas. The sky is a gas, alas. In our eyes, our view, the picture plane, the sky is contained only by visible edges, and so the sky, in art, can be held by a container, so to speak. The sky is represented by that which falls or flies or passes through it. Okay.

Do a 3D artwork in any medium involving the idea of the visible sky being contained by the limits of your peripheral vision. Can the sky be held in a bowl or a box? How will it feel like sky and not just contained air? Are there other ways of portraying the visible limits of the sky without it being surrounded by a container?

Think about the sky being signified by the creatures and objects that pass through it. How could they be portrayed, therefore representing the sky?

Do your own brainstorm/free-write sort of thing, and see what you find in your own words.

Cactus

Cactus elements – Prickly, needles, spike, smooth, fuzzy, flowers, fruit, cactus pears, barrels, flat pads, ridges
Cactus concepts – Character, succulent, efficient, hardy, sturdy, desert, survivors in rough country
Other things – Hollow, shallow roots

Shapes and Edges

Do a semi-abstracted artwork based on the shapes of cactus pads, in any medium. Use one or more of any type of cactus (or any succulent plant) in your piece. Aim for about a 50% representational/pictorial quality, so that 'cactus' is clearly a recognizable subject matter. Include approximately 10% of other pictorial elements, including the background. At least two of your cactus pads must go off the edge of the picture plane, if you are creating a two-dimensional piece.

Character

Cactus have personality, more than most plants, it seems. Do a portrait of an individual cactus, using the cactus concepts and visual elements from above. You can portray the cactus as a plant or you can give it more of an anthropomorphic or zoomorphic character. Do a series of portraits, or a group portrait of various cacti.

Create a western scene, starring cactus. Include every classic western thing you can possibly think of, and then some. Think of the desert southwest, Old Mexico, the western sunset, coyotes, the lonesome notes of a solitary harmonica. Push the imagery as far as you can go, and cram it all into the picture plane, or the sculptural form or grouping. Make the artwork completely and wonderfully absurd in its excess. Have fun.

Xeriscaping

Design a drought-resistant lawn and you will never have to mow again. Having lived twice in the desert, I have had the pleasure of seeing creativity in action when it comes to front yards, road dividers, civic plazas and city parks. And as inspiration for this subject, I will now include this book's solitary haiku:

Lawns of bowling balls
gas meters and whirligigs
xeriscaped in bliss

Design a road median, or other compact public space, using the following materials; rock, glass, wood, and at least one kitchen implement. Use any amount and interpretation of those materials you like. For example; terrarium pebbles, three big gray rocks, yellow stained-glass scraps, two drinking glasses, a few dozen popsicle sticks, a colander and five mismatched forks. Don't forget to add some cactus to the mix.

Design a front lawn with the following guidelines and including these materials; five species of cactus, four kinds of non-plant ground cover, an animal statue of any kind, the color blue, one triangle, two rows and three circles.

Design a fence or other structure based on cactus. Actually, fences of ocotillo and other cactus are quite common in Mexico and the U.S. Southwest. Do a drawing or a maquette, or make an actual structure (this will keep you busy). Include at least three different types of cactus, although past this limit you may also include other succulent plants if you like. Base your idea on a well-known architectural style such as art deco, gothic or mid-century modern; anything but classic adobe.

Finding Inspiration in the Urban World

Windows

Window elements – Glass, panes, tinted, stained, reflective, frosted
Window concepts – Looking in, looking out, open, closed, broken, window shopping, different ways of opening
Window things – Windowsills, window boxes, shutters, blinds, shades, curtains, screens, awnings, displays, signs
Types of actual windows – Double-hung, casement, sliding, top-hinged, room windows, storm windows, screen windows, storefront windows, car, train, bus windows, picture windows, bay windows, oven windows, dryer windows, stained-glass windows

Window coverings

Real window coverings include curtains made of fabric, blinds in vinyl, shutters in wood, and awnings in metal.

Inventive window coverings could include anything strung and hanging like beaded curtains, one giant pompom over each window, blinds of pencils woven with twine, shutters of coconut shell, curtains designed like items of clothing or giant pot holders, or a transparent plastic awning, which would let in the sun, but keep out the rain.

Design and/or create a set of window coverings for a room. Use elements of the view outside, or reflect the theme or use of the room. You can also add meaning to your window coverings, besides paying attention to the materials and visual aesthetics.

Panes and frames

Do a painting on glass. Find an old window (thrift stores, flea markets, salvage yards). Treat the window frame as the painting frame and finish it any way you like. Paint on the windowpanes. You can play with the idea of it being a window and paint the view outside or the scene inside. You can also ignore the fact that it is a window, and simply consider it an interesting painting surface. With multiple panes you can do unrelated little paintings, a series of related pictures, a continuing story (like in the comics), or one large painting over the whole window.

Do a weaving or a mixed-media piece in an open window frame where all of the glass has been removed. Use the window frame as the supporting structure for your art. Again, you can work with the idea of it having once been an actual window, or you can simply create your piece using the material and aesthetics of the frame.

Faux stained-glass

Create a stained-glass window in any other medium besides glass. A few possible ideas:

- Glass beads strung on wire and supported by a frame. Use black or metallic beads as the solder.

- A mixed-media piece also supported by a frame. Use black or metallic yarn or wire for the solder.

- A faux stained-glass quilt using black or metallic thread or binding tape for the solder.

- Any two-dimensional work on paper, canvas or panel would make a fine, albeit opaque, faux stained-glass window. For transparency, use acetate sheets as your surface.

Window display

Create a window display for an actual or imagined business or store. This can be a painting, drawing, print, arranged photograph, diorama or installation piece (or even a sculpture or a knitted piece). A collage might be the perfect thing for this. Think about the signage, lettering and placement of the objects in the window as a whole composition. Include the following things in your window display; the name of the business, a sign with the hours, a minimum of five objects related to the business, two predominant colors, one accent color, at least one figure of some kind (it doesn't have to be human), and a small set of anything hanging from the ceiling.

Create a window display for a made-up holiday or sale at a store. Choose a type of store and a holiday. A few examples would be:

- A sock store on Squirrel Eve

- A robot store and International Snow Holiday

- A store that sells wood pieces and scraps celebrating Cups o' Nothing Week

Remember that you must entice window shoppers to come on in and do their holiday shopping in this particular store. Decide on a few of your own random guidelines first and then go from there.

Window box

Create a window box, the container itself. What else can it be other than a plain wooden or plastic box? Could it also be a series of smaller boxes or buckets? How would they be held together or attached to each other? How would the box or containers be mounted outside a window? Think about embellishments for the window box, for aesthetic purposes and/or for suggesting a meaning.

Fill the window box, but not with the usual flowers or plants. Think of the window box as a sort of diorama or mini-installation with sculptural possibilities. Some ideas are:

- Imply a garden without using plants, real or fake.

- Make a window-aquarium, but without using water or living things.

- Fill it with abstracted fake flowers that you make from any material. Plant them in anything but soil.

• Create an absurd farm scene; a comedy of plastic cows, rows of tiny fake crops and alien spaceships.

Faces

Do a portrait, or a series of portraits, of faces pressed up against various windowpanes. The face, or faces, may either be looking in or looking out. Pay attention to the flattening of facial features and the fog of warm breath on the glass. Think about what the person or persons may be feeling when looking through the window. Looking in a window typically signifies curiosity, being left out and voyeurism. Looking out often means loneliness, longing, and dreaming of the view; a desire to leave.

Do a portrait, or a series of portraits, of faces in the reflection of the glass. Pay attention to the reflective qualities of the scene, transparencies, and implied meanings made by the layers of what can be seen in a reflection.

Kitties sitting in the window are a common scene. What else could there be perched on a windowsill looking out? How amusing, strange, scary and/or beautiful is it? Is it pressed up against the glass and slightly flattened?

Windows looking out free-write example:

Stare and stare through the window's glare searching for distant horizons, way over there. A glance on the chance for the weather in a dance, is it snowing, is it glowing, is it raining, are there stains out on the street, isn't it sweet, gonna dream of leaving going out in only daydreams. A pin for the pondering, no sin in thinking yonder, pacing windowsills with fingers set on sliding down hand rails. This is restless, this is pining, this is being pinned...

What images can you see from this free-writing sample?

Do your own brainstorming, free-writing and/or word association on the subject of looking out the window. Think of one of the following things to begin your writing session; the outside world, the view, the sense of distance, eyes being the windows of the soul, what you see when you look out a window.

What images have you come up with from your own writing?

Depict what you are seeing from any of your word images or mine.

Create anything that you want in any medium, in any format, and without restrictions, unless you would like to set some of your own guidelines before you start.

More window inspiration

Here are some other ideas that you can use as a basis for artistic creativity. You may also combine anything from below with another exercise in any chapter to make something original.

- The breeze. Open the window to let in a breeze. What comes in on the breeze? The idea of the cross-breeze.

- Windows in disrepair. Broken, patched, boarded up, gone completely.

- As seen from a distance, the patterns and rows of windows on a building, or maybe a stack of windows at the home repair store.

- Invent a window. New ways of opening and closing, or maybe you could create a revolving window. Picture the use of the window, invent one on paper and build a model.

Traffic Lights

Traffic light elements – Green, yellow, red, flashing, circles, arrows, blinking, metal, pole, wire, glass
Traffic light concepts – Changing meaning; go, go that way, stop, wait, caution, urban traffic, a one traffic light town
Traffic light situations – On a pole, hanging from a wire, one-sided, four-sided, bulb out, glass broken

Abstraction

Create an abstracted piece using only the following elements: The colors green, red, yellow, white and black. You may also use metallic paints in these colors or other metallic materials (depending on your medium). Use the shapes of disks, circles, rectangles and arrows, with these shapes covering at least 75% of your composition. A maximum of 25% of the piece may either be a solid field or a soft, vague, blurred, just-barely-hinted-at background scene. This can be expressed in any medium or form. It could even be a beaded sculpture with wires or knotted in yarn with buttons and feathers.

Scenery

Illustrate one or more of the following settings. Portray the mood of the scene, and not just how it looks on the surface. You may include some abstract elements, or you may go for pure representationalism.

- That solo middle-of the-night-on-a-deserted-street flashing yellow light
- Rush hour in the busy downtown of a big city
- A lazy summer afternoon in a one traffic light town
- Any other scene where the traffic light is the main character

Meaning

Design a new system of traffic signage based on the questions in the point below. Include one of these new traffic lights in a scene. Set a particular mood, depending on the meaning of the new traffic signal.

- What would traffic lights of other colors such as blue or orange mean?
- What new symbols could traffic lights use besides hand, man walking, or arrow?
- What different words could there be for pedestrian signals besides walk, wait or stop?

Invention

Design and/or create a new traffic light for any of the following purposes:

- An intergalactic traffic light
- For the middle of nowhere here on earth
- For the only bathroom in a crowded household
- For a busy kitchen at a popular restaurant
- For dogs at a dog park
- For a public swimming pool or ice rink
- At a department store during the holiday season.
- For the dance floor

Subway

Subway elements – Color, letter, number-coded systems and maps, trains, trolleys, tracks, wires, third rail, tunnels, turnstiles, stairs, escalators, signs, metal, plastic, tile, wood, concrete
Subway concepts – Moving people, ride, commute, go, underground world, busy city
Subway things – Sound, smell, noise, speed, rush, schedules, tokens, passes

In London, as in some other places, the subway means an underground walkway, often beneath a busy intersection in a city. Here I am using the New York City definition, since this is where I was born, with subway meaning trains on tracks running below the ground. In London this is called the Underground. In other places it is referred to as the Metro, or maybe by its particular name such as the T in Boston. They are very big on abbreviating names in Boston, and T is about at short as it gets.

Maps and signage

Design a signage system for an imaginary subway; for entrances and exits at stations, a coding system for the different train lines, printed schedules for each line (or a master schedule), and tickets, tokens and monthly passes.

Design a map for the above system. Decide on names for the lines, stations and destinations. While you are at it, invent a new way of folding this very same map.

If you live somewhere without a subway system, design one for your village, town, city or county. Follow the instructions in the above two points. Use real names from your own locale.

Use real or imagined subway map elements in an abstracted artwork, any medium. Include the following; station names, linear elements, track graphics. Limit yourself to five colors (and their variations), plus black and white, and individual line numbers, codes or icons. You may include any other subway element in this piece as well, but keep it subtle.

Subway cars

Paint, draw or create train-model-size subway cars based on any of the following visual design ideas:

- Carousel animals, or mythological creatures
- Other modes of transportation such as cars, boats, trucks, airplanes or rockets
- Seed pods, plant forms or food items.

Paint, draw or create train-model-size subway cars based on any of the following functions:

- A dinner and movie car
- The poetry slam car
- A little kids' playtime car
- A create-more-time concept car for the way-too-busy
- The train-buff club car

Abstraction

Do a completely abstract work based on the sounds and/or smells of the subway. Do not include any recognizable objects. Use as many colors as you need.

Do a semi-abstract piece based on the movement of the trains; the speed, the rush, the screeching to a stop. Make the piece at least 50% abstract, but include at least 10% recognizable subject matter such as a hint of subway car. Limit your color palette to the minimum of what you need to express the movement of subway trains.

You may also do a piece similar to the above, based on the movement of people in the subway.

Portray the view out the window of a moving subway car as a blur.

Use the linear elements of the subway as the basis for an abstract piece, such as tracks, third rails, wires and pipes. Limit yourself to a maximum of 10% recognizable subject matter. Include at least three compositional triangles.

Portraiture

Do a portrait, or a series of portraits, or a group portrait of passengers focusing on the following things:

- The rows of feet lined up along the subway car floor. This works best if the car has two long rows of facing seats.

- Subway riders wearing hats. It's almost always an interesting variety, and they lend much personality.

- The hands of the passengers; on their laps, reading, fidgeting, holding things, folded.

- Where the gazes of the passengers lead to; closed eyes, lost out the window, flirting across the aisle.

Posters

Design a poster, or a series of posters, for subway stations and/or the inside the subway cars. Posters are used for advertising products, services, exhibits, concerts, and community events. They are also used for subway system announcements. For each thing that is advertised, decide on a limited color scheme, typography usage and graphic elements, which include many of the basic visual elements. Keep it visually clean and simple.

Create more of a fine art piece based on the above poster; where the edges are a little blurry, the meaning somewhat obscured, the words are almost gone, and the edges of the colors are not all so crisp.

Subway stations

Design or invent one or more stations for The State of Being subway line. Each station is named for a state of mind or emotion such as elation, hysteria, contentment, anxiety, and/or hopefulness. Designate a color code for each station.

Design or invent a set of stations with the theme of each one being a different place, country or culture from around the world.

Design or invent a set of stations for places where there would really be no subway such as the middle of any possible nowhere, a small isolated town, or under the ocean. What would the stations be like? Consider their function.

Design a station for pure aesthetics. Pick a main color, a secondary color and an accent color (60%, 30% and 10% approximately). Choose materials, lines, masses and visual themes for the floor, walls, ceiling, benches, lighting, exits, signage (assuming that the ticket windows and shops are upstairs). For example; bright mid-tone green, blue and purple for anything painted. Light green, blue and purple for the tiled areas of the walls. The floors are dark shades of green and blue tiles. Patterns of diamonds, triangles and single thin stripes dominate as design elements. The ceilings are mostly a light blue. Pendant lamps are a medium green painted metal. And so on.

Design or create individual tiles, mosaic signage or a mosaic mural for a subway station wall. Include elements of where that particular station is located into the design. For example; a mosaic for a station in a park could include leaves, trees and squirrels. If the station is near an ice cream shop, include graphics of cones and various toppings. Tiles for a station near the waterfront might have fish and boat images pressed into them. Where is your station located?

Abandoned Factories

Abandoned factory elements – Smokestacks, chimneys, bricks, cinderblocks, peeling paint, gears, wheels, walls, broken windows, chain-link fence, wood palettes, massive, solid, hollow

Abandoned factory concepts – Old industrial city, working history, future gentrification, failure, changes in economy, empty

Abandoned factory free-write

Bits of bricks on sidewalk sticks a gated fence a chain-link mess, you have no idea the life that once revolved around here, where this is now nowhere to be found, torn-up stuff on the ground falling all around a dented wall a metal fall and locks on everything they used to sing, what did they make what did they create is it all on vacation now permanently away a broken broke holiday, but the pieces of bricks they stay...

Do a brainstorming, free-writing and/or word association session starting with any of the abandoned factory elements or concepts listed above.

What images do you see in your own writing? What can you make from what you now see?

Imagine a ghost factory, maybe on the outskirts of a ghost town. Create simple or complex scenes using imagery from your writing, and/or mine. Think about the ethereal spirits that labor inside the walls. What are they doing? What does the building look like, both inside and out? What do they make at this factory?

Patterns and geometry

Look at the geometrical structure of an old factory. Look at it from different perspectives, and find an angle that is visually pleasing to you. If there are multiple smokestacks and chimneys, notice the pattern, if any.

Create a semi-abstract piece in any medium based on the silhouette, geometry, angles and lines of the factory. Have the artwork be recognizable as an abandoned factory, but you can take liberties with the realism/abstraction factor from there. Think about smoke, haziness, striking sunlight and/or elements from the factory's surroundings when working on your piece.

Create a completely abstract artwork based only on the pure visual elements from your chosen factory. Combine three large flat areas of outside wall, five to eight windows, one to four smokestacks and at least seven lines in any form or usage to make your composition. If working in color, have your palette be at least 90% of the actual factory coloring. The other 10% is up to you.

Create a representational work. Have the geometry and structure of the factory be a key visual element in your piece. Include at least one type of pattern, such as bricks or a row of smokestacks.

Sociology

An abandoned factory is not only an empty structure; it has a past, maybe some kind of a future, and definitely a human story. When a factory closes what happens to the workers, their families and the surrounding neighborhoods?

Do a portrait, or a series, of former factory personnel. Show their own personal story on each of their faces. These can be real or imagined people.

Portray a scene from the day that the real or imagined factory closed its doors.

Do a plein-air painting or drawing, or a series, detailing little vignettes focusing on the edges of the factory property. This might be where the chain-link fence meets the sidewalk weeds, or the shuttered gate with the sign saying "closed".

Portray the natural decay of the factory building and its various parts. Do a series showing this decay in a time-lapse format.

Do a drawing or a maquette about the interesting things you envision could be developed from the factory shell and the property.

Design a factory

What might the exterior of these possible factories look like? Have the design reflect both the practical and whimsical aspects of its manufacturing purpose.

- A toy musical instrument factory, with the smokestacks looking like trumpets
- A boredom factory (maker of products for when things get too exciting), where everything is beige
- A factory for imaginary bicycles
- A sandwich factory
- A bottle and jar factory
- A button factory
- A surprise factory

Finding Inspiration
in Everyday Household Items

Pillows

Pillow elements – Soft, scrunchy, stuffing, cases, bolsters, round, square, rectangular, velvet, cotton, satin, fake fur, colors, patterns, zippers, trims, tassels
Pillow concepts – Comfort, huggable, to prop yourself up, decorative, sleep, nap, relax

Pillow designs

Make real functional sofa-type pillows, but in a completely new design that you have never seen before. Expand your thinking on pillow shapes, surface materials and stuffing. If you cannot think of anything, then use ideas from one of the other chapters in this book, such as pillows inspired by seashells or breakfast food items.

Design mystery pillows with multiple pockets, zippers, folded fabric, attachments, enclosures, or pillows hidden inside of other pillows.

Create a few pillows out of metal, wood, glass or any other hard material. Make them look very much like soft pillows with seams and creases. Maybe add a little trim to the sides or tassels for the corners.

Two-dimensional

Do a painting, drawing or print with pillows as your subject matter, in a realistic manner.

Do two of the above two-dimensional pieces, but portray three pillows each time. Use a very limited palette for the first one, such as a range of reds and oranges only, including the background. Do the second piece in as many colors as possible.

Do an abstract piece based on a pile of pillows. Pay attention to line, form and pattern.

Sleep and dreams

Portray a scene from one of your dreams. Do this in any medium, in any way you like, to best express the dream.

What do pillows dream about while you are sleeping? Portray a pillow's dream.

Pillow fight

Portray a pillow fight. This can be the classic pillow fight involving people, or maybe it is a scene of pillows fighting among themselves. Work in any medium, in any format, and without restrictions.

Create or portray a pillow that is fighting with itself.

Pillowcases

Make pillowcases for your bed pillows with scenes from actual dreams you have had. You can also portray something that you wish to dream about.

Design a new type of pillowcase for a bed pillow. Think of function and/ or aesthetics, such as a pocket for tissues or with a surface pattern you would like, but is not available in the stores.

Un-pillow-like

Do a painting, drawing, maquette or an installation piece based on pillows behaving in un-pillow-like ways. Work with one of the following ideas:

- A typically cold, hard structure made mostly of pillows such as a bridge, a locomotive engine or a castle
- Warrior pillows, soldier pillows, hunting pillows, bully pillows, pillows being anything but warm, soft and comforting
- Pre-historic pillows
- Pillows from outer space

Shoes

Shoe elements – Leather, canvas, rubber, laces, eyelets, heels, tongue, toe, sole, arch, pointy, square, round, strappy, chunky, style, color
Shoe types – Tap, ballet, slippers, sneakers, flip flops, boots, walking shoes, running shoes, ice skates, roller skates
Other shoe things – Shoe polish, shoehorn, sizes, shoeboxes, socks, feet, heels, toes
Shoe meanings – Shoes are a means of travel and therefore freedom, they are tires for your feet. New shoes are a cause for celebration.
Why this is household stuff – Because shoes can often be found lying around the house

Portraiture

Shoes have character, and therefore deserve portraits of their own. Do a portrait of shoes in any medium. Work in a representational or semi-representational fashion. Make sure that the subject is recognizable as being shoes. Choose one idea from each of the two sections below and combine to make your portrait.

1. A solitary shoe
2. A pair of shoes (matched or not)
3. A formal grouping of shoes
4. An informal pile of shoes

A. With scenery in the background
B. With drapery in the background
C. With a color wash in the background
D. With a hint of the proud owner in the background

Assemblage

Make an assemblage piece with actual shoes and parts of shoes. Use your own worn-out shoes, or shoes that you find at thrift-stores, yard sales and flea markets. Include one or more of the following ideas into your assemblage:

Add other items to your assemblage; anything from ribbons or twigs to plumbing parts or lemon peels. Anything.

Work purely from your own sense of aesthetics, completely disregarding meaning.

Work with any of the shoe meanings from above, or any other serious or humorous concept. If you are stuck concerning meaning, do a free-writing session and see what thoughts come to you.

Non-humans in shoes

Portray animals, real or imagined, wearing people shoes. What kind of shoes would they wear?

Portray inanimate objects wearing people shoes. A few examples would be; a fire hydrant wearing fishing boots, or a cala lily wearing a ballet slipper. Or maybe the fire hydrant is the one wearing the ballet slippers.

Design or create shoes for animals and/or inanimate objects. Think about function, as well as style.

Do a small series of formal portraits of animals and/or inanimate objects wearing their new custom-designed shoes. Have the figures be standing in front of scenery or a classically draped wall. You may also portray these figures in action, with their shoes playing an important role in the story.

Body parts

Do a portrait using the same idea as those earlier well-known produce portraits. These were human faces constructed with images of fruits and vegetables. Create a human or animal face or figure using shoe parts, especially those named after body parts such as; heel, tongue, toe, sole, arch and eye(let).

Composition

Use various shoe elements, parts and things from the lists at the beginning of this section in a composition. For example: Combine eyelets, flip-flop straps, roller skate wheels, shoe polish and feet in a composition. You may work in any style.

Do an abstraction based on any or all of the following elements; pointy, square, round, strappy, chunky, leather, canvas and/or rubber.

Do an abstraction based on the sound of active flip flops, ice skates or tap shoes.

Active shoes

Create a series of vignettes of a pair of shoes out on their own as they see the world, or at least different corners of the neighborhood.

Portray dancing shoes dancing together, or other specialty shoes doing their own special thing. For example: Fishing boots fishing, ice skates skating, tennis shoes playing tennis.

Shoehorn

Do a still-life of a shoe with a horn, either a beep-beep horn or a rhino-type horn.

Create a musical horn shaped like a shoe.

Design a shoe that looks something like a musical horn.

The original diorama

Create a diorama about the shoe shopping experience; with the sheer frustration or the absolute joy expressed in an actual cardboard shoebox. You may also work outside the box, but make sure that all the pieces are attached or in proximity to the shoebox. You may use any material you like, and in any style.

As more of a challenge, create the above diorama, but limit yourself to only two materials of your choice (not including the box). For example; glass and paper, which would include stained glass pieces, mirror bits, glass beads, small jars, etc., and paper of any kind including cardboard. Two more examples would be paint and yarn, or metal and plastic.

Create a diorama using any materials, limited or not, depending on your sense of aesthetics, about how new shoes are feeling while in the box waiting to be taken home. You may also portray old shoes about to be exchanged or left behind at the shoe store. Consider both ideas from the shoes' point of view.

The Bath

Bath elements – Tub, shower, tile, porcelain, shiny, tap, spigot, faucet, water, steam, bubble, rubber duck, soap, washcloth, terry cloth, overflow, bath mat, shower curtain
Bath concepts – Hot, warm, tepid, cold, dirty, clean, wet
Bath meanings – Cleansing, renewing, soak away troubles, physically and emotionally healing

Bath tile

Design or create individual tiles for your ideal bath. Think about the color, texture and shape of the tiles. Are they made of ceramic, glass or something else? Is there an image imprinted on them? Is something etched into the surface?

In what pattern would your tiles be installed? Would the pattern be stripes, checks, a spiral, or something more complex?

Design or create a mosaic mural using bath tile. You can, of course, go for a water theme of any kind, or you can do something that has absolutely nothing to do with the idea of the bath.

Bath scenes

Think of those famous classical, romantic paintings of bath scenes from an earlier era. Create your own bath scene using guidelines from any of the following points:

Portray one solo figure in the bath. Create an ambience using a limited palette of color, reflective of the mood of the bather, which can be anything you choose. Have the background be a wallpaper pattern, also reflective of the same mood. If the bather is figuratively steaming, as well as literally, then have the colors be mostly reds and other hot colors and the wallpaper pattern be something like little red-hot irons.

Portray two or three figures, interacting with each other or not. Have the tub be outdoors with scenery of any kind receding into the distance. Place three or four random objects on the ground in front of the bathtub.

Portray a group of seven or more figures in a pool-like bath in one of those classic interior scenes, only do a modern version. Be liberal with your use of drapery. Use as many colors as you like.

Still-life

Create a still-life based on bath items such as soap, towels and faucets. A pile of towels can make for an interesting composition. The surface of a bar of soap can be quite lovely and complex with the light hitting it just so. An arrangement of shiny plumbing parts could also be very intriguing. Work in a perfect square if your medium is two-dimensional.

Shower curtains

Create a shower curtain from unusual, but relatively waterproof, materials, with a set of matching hooks. Have the design be inspired by the materials used, as well as the idea of the bath.

Design a non-typical shower curtain pattern or scene. Have the picture or pattern be as un-bath-like as possible.

Design a shower curtain on a bath or water theme, but have it be very different from any you have ever seen before.

Design a shower curtain using only color and geometry. Have it be different from, but compliment, any tile patterns you may have designed.

Abstraction

Create a completely abstract piece based on at least three of the visual elements (see the earlier chapter on the visual elements), and the ideas of flowing water, sitting water, steam, fog, haze, dampness and/or drips.

Plumbing

Construct a miniature plumbing system, such as a small fountain or aqueduct. You may use anything or any material that conducts water.

Make a construction of any kind for any reason, using mostly plumbing and bath parts; plugs, faucets, pipes, etc. Go to the plumbing aisle of your local hardware store. You will see all kinds of intriguing items from which you can create other things.

Think about the view from inside the pipes. Imagine being very small and travelling through the pipes in a tiny boat. Depict this intra-plumbing journey in one scene or more.

Do an abstraction based on the flow and splash of water as it fills the tub in preparation for a bath.

Do an abstraction based on the whirlpool and suction of the water as it goes down the drain after the bath.

Soak your troubles away

They say that taking a bath will soak away your troubles, but where do those troubles go? What does a trouble look like? Does it have a recognizable face? Are those troubles pictorialized by tiny little abstract objects?

Do a portrait of a trouble in any form you can imagine that a trouble would be, if represented by itself.

Create a scene where your troubles are literally being washed away, dissolved or transformed by the bath water.

Bubbles

Do a self-portrait as reflected in multitudes of bath bubbles, maybe even covered in bubbles, as well.

Do a representational painting or drawing of a few bubbles in close detail. Pay special attention to the transparencies and reflections.

Make bubbles in any three-dimensional medium. For example; wire mesh bubbles, blown-glass bubbles, crocheted bubbles (maybe in bubble colored yarn with metallic glints), or even wooden bubbles.

Dream tub

Design your dream bathtub. Consider the following things; the shape, depth and color of the tub itself, if it is raised or sunken into the floor, and where in the room it might be located. Is there a window or a skylight? What is the tub itself made of, and are there any special coating materials? Are there plants nearby? What sort of lighting is there? Is there a color scheme to the room? Be as elaborate as you desire. This is your ideal bathtub, nobody else's.

Eyeglasses

Eyeglass elements – Frames, plastic, wire, lenses, nose-bridge, hinges, folding, glasses case

Eyeglasses concepts and meanings – Intelligence, professional, bookworm, nerd, desire to see, vision, misplaced glasses (because you can't see to find them)

Eyeglasses types – Spectacles, monocles, bifocals, trifocals, sunglasses, magnifying glasses, binoculars, opera glasses, x-ray glasses

Why this is household stuff – Because eyeglasses can often be found lying around the house

Abstraction

Do an abstract piece based on eyeglass forms such as the frames, the lenses, the nose-bridge and hinges. Portray multiple pairs of glasses with no more than 25% realism or recognizable parts. Pay attention to the elements of shine and reflection, as well as the distortion as seen through eyeglass lenses at a slight distance. Limit your palette to the colors that you actually see in and around the glasses that you are abstractly portraying.

Construction

Go to the thrift store or flea market and buy a bunch of old eyeglass frames, with or without the lenses. Go to your home or studio and make something. Make a tangled mess, or make a solid and well-ordered structure. Build a tower, a boat, a flying machine or any other construction. Include a few other materials, especially for attaching or tying frames together, but no more than four other things. Have the frames and lenses be at least 80% of your construction.

Double Portrait

Create a double portrait, or a series of double portraits of people with and without glasses.

Do the same as the above, but with portraits of animals or inanimate objects.

Style

Design and/or create new eyeglasses. Think about material, color, function and embellishments. Consider how the style reflects the situation or occasion listed below:

- Seasonal eyeglasses; winter, spring, summer, fall
- Eyeglasses designed especially for certain holidays
- Nature-themed eyeglasses
- Eyeglasses for pets
- Eyeglasses for imaginary creatures

Eyeglass cases

Design an eyeglass case for any of the above eyeglasses that you may have created. Think about surface pattern.

Design a completely new type of eyeglass case, maybe with a new hinge system, or with pockets or other functions.

Examination of details

Portray something magnified or seen through binoculars, so that it is obvious that the subject is being observed at close range.

Do a mixed composition combining the concepts of both near and far at same time. Do not do something as simple as a close object or figure with a distant landscape, but something more complex, with both ideas intertwined.

Rose-colored glasses

Portray anything as seen through rose-colored, or any other color, glasses. Does the color filter change the mood of what you are portraying?

Portray something as seen through distorted lenses, or through eyeglasses that are not made for you. Be careful not to hurt your eyes. Just take a very quick look and re-create what you saw from memory.

Create an abstract piece based on this distortion and color-shift, but depict no recognizable objects.

Bowls

Bowl elements – Round, oval, vessel, full, empty, upside-down, stacked, nestled, inside, outside, convex, concave, rim, shiny, matte, ringed, ceramic, glass, Pyrex
Bowl concepts – Container, comfort food, love, abundance

Bowl forms

Create new forms and designs for bowls. Consider both aesthetics and function. Bowls already come in so many wonderful shapes and forms. The challenge will be to come up with something that you have never seen before. Maybe the bowl can be inspired by something in nature, or designed with pure geometry used in a new way. Focus on any or all of the following:

- The bowl body; this would be the container part of the bowl – think about the three-dimensional shape, the thickness of the wall, and the depth or height of the bowl

- Stems and bases; think about how the bowl might sit on a table

- Materials; what is the bowl made of? Does it need to be ceramic, wood or glass or can it be made of some unusual material? Could the bowl be made of a composite of different materials?

- Rim embellishments and form

Surface patterns and textures

For example: A geometric bowl that is trapezoidal in shape, has a chunky triangular base and is made of white stoneware. A pattern of diamonds could be loosely etched into the surface of the bowl, giving it some texture. The base could be a soft yellow, the body glazed an olive green, with the very top of the rim bordered with a stripe of violet. Simple, but different.

Nesting

Do a two-dimensional piece on the idea of a bowl being a nest for birds or other nesting creatures.

Create an actual, functional bowl based on the design of a bird's nest.

Portray a bowl, or set of bowls, nesting as of they were birds. Call the piece "Nesting Bowls".

Play with the idea of nesting bowls as seen from overhead. Do you see the concentric circles, edges, patterns and highlights? Use these visual elements to express something that has nothing to do with the idea of nesting.

Anti-container

Design or create a bowl, or set of bowls, that cannot contain. Do not make the typical colander, but something else. Think about what it is that is leaking through, draining out or getting away. This could be a conceptual piece, either a two-dimensional portrayal or an actual bowl with a serious problem.

Love and abundance

Bowls offer love, hope, comfort and abundance. Even though bowls contain, they are also open at the top. They are holding and giving at the same time.

Think of bowls as cupped hands full of stuff, an offering, a gift. Create or depict a bowl made of hands or hand-like forms.

What could be inside of a bowl besides some belly-warming soup? Could it contain something else besides liquids or objects? Maybe the bowl could hold an idea or an emotion. Create or depict such a bowl and its contents.

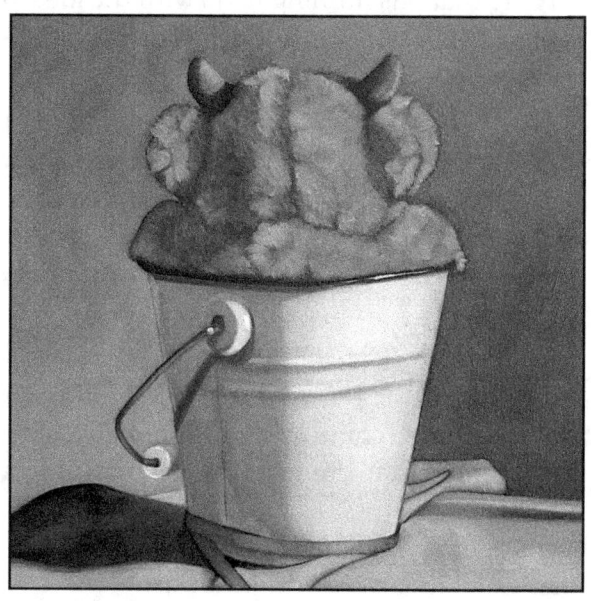

Finding Inspiration
in Domestic Routines

Doing Laundry

Laundry elements – Washing machines, dryers, baskets, detergent, bleach, clothing, towels, linens, lint, laundry lines, hangers
Laundry concepts – Wet, dry, piles, folded, shiny, fluffy, squeaky clean, laundry list, money laundering
Other laundry things – The laundromat environment, sound, vibration, quarters

Laundry piles

Paint or draw a pile of dirty laundry. Choose clothing of similar colors, like blues and greens, with maybe one orange sock for contrast. Make a really gorgeous composition out of it. Work in any style you choose.

Think about the possible meanings that can found in a large pile of laundry. It could mean laziness, maybe it's a sign of being too busy, or it could be something else altogether. Design or create an installation involving any meaning you might find in piles of laundry.

Window

Do a portrait as seen in the reflection of a washer or dryer window, either at a laundromat or at home. Include at least one other reflected item outside of the machine, as well as something else (real or imaginary) as seen through the washer or dryer window that is inside the machine.

Portray something spinning inside the washer or dryer as seen through the window, with at least one still item also being reflected by that window.

Portray somebody or something trapped inside the washer or dryer looking sort of circular, reflective and vague, as seen through the window. They may be tumbling or not.

Laundromat design

Design a complete laundromat based on one of the following themes:

- Tropical resort
- Blizzard at the local train station
- Fun with reptiles
- International drums
- Vegetable bin
- Simple aesthetics, focusing on a color scheme and a geometric shape, such as pink, silver, brown and ovals

Neptune

Depict the laundromat, or your laundry room, as an underwater scene. Include fish, other sea creatures, marine plant life, coral and/or rocks.

Design or create a laundromat aquarium. Instead of the typical castles, have little washers, dryers and laundry baskets for the fish to swim through.

Sew or construct machine-washable fabric fish out of old clothing, linens, bath mats and so on.

Laundry lines

I have always seen laundry lines as aesthetically pleasing, for some reason. Once I painted a pair of yellow rubber gloves on a laundry line in San Francisco. I called the painting Tuesday Morning (http://alexalev.com/book-references.html). An elderly woman, a few houses over, used to hang all kinds of things out to dry. I often found her laundry line to be very interesting.

Do a painting or drawing of an actual laundry line with wash hanging out to dry. You may do this in any style you choose, from representational to completely abstract.

Depict or create a laundry line in any two or three-dimensional medium. Hang anything you like from the line, but give it some kind of a story or sense of inquiry, as if whatever it is that is hanging out to dry has its own reason for being there.

Create a three-dimensional piece made predominantly of laundry line materials; cords, pulleys and clothespins.

Spinning

Think of all the things that spin at once in a laundromat; washers, dryers and overhead fans. Most likely, they are spinning in different directions and at different speeds.

Do an abstract two-dimensional piece based on all the spinning tubs, blades and baskets at the laundromat. Have the object recognizability factor be in the 0% to 50% range. Use many different types of line in your composition. Limit your colors to laundromat colors.

Create an abstract three-dimensional piece with an abundance of spinning parts.

Sounds and vibrations

Do a completely abstract piece based on the sounds and physical vibrations of a busy laundromat. Work with pure visual elements only, without any recognizable objects to portray non-visual sensations. Think about what kinds of lines, shapes and colors the sounds and vibrations make.

If you like, include the smell of detergent to your visual interpretation of a laundromat. What color does detergent and bleach smell like? Does the smell have a texture?

Folding

Do an assemblage or mixed-media piece about the idea of folding. Use any materials you like, but have the main focus be something that is folded; purely about aesthetics and material concerns.

Portray something that is representative of a real object. Think about why the subject or object is being folded, and include some kind of meaning to the image.

Lint

Do a representational still-life of a ball of lint. Try to replicate the exact texture of the lint ball on the two-dimensional surface.

Make a sculptural piece that is at least 90% made of laundry lint. It is helpful to have access to a home dryer to collect lint. Work in any color or colors of lint that you can gather. Make something that has absolutely nothing to do with laundry.

Eating Breakfast

Breakfast elements – Table, chair, spoon, fork, knife, plate, bowl, glass, mug, pitcher

Breakfast foods – Toast, eggs, cereal, fruit, juice, coffee, tea, oatmeal, pancakes, bagels, muffins, bacon, sausage, typical breakfast foods from other cultures

Breakfast concepts – Typical, traditional, morning, hungry, early, sunrise, sleepy, the act of eating, newspaper, pajamas, rush, breaking the fast, first meal of the day, sustenance

Citrus peels

Collect and dry citrus peels from any kind of citrus fruit. When they are completely dried, make something out of them that is at least 80% citrus peel.

Peel any citrus fruit in one long piece. Tangerines are easiest for this task. Arrange the peel into an interesting pose, and do a representational portrayal of it.

Making a creative breakfast

Make a batch of pancake batter and divide it into a few different bowls. Add a few drops of food coloring to each bowl, so that you now have bowls of different colors of batter. Next, make multi-color pancakes with the batter.

Arrange whole and cut pieces of fruit into a sculptural object; using the fruit like building blocks.

Still-life

Do a still-life of breakfast items. However, keep the subject matter to no more than two types of items. For example; five pieces of fruit, one fork and two spoons (fruit and utensils), or a pitcher of juice, a cup of coffee and a pile of napkins (beverages and napkins).

Photograph breakfast scenes, staged or informal, in black and white. Bring the photos into photo editing software, and play with various settings and filters, so that the images look like breakfast noir.

Abstraction

Do an abstract piece based on the breakfast table, but have no more than a 20% recognizability factor. Use all or some of the colors of the items on the table. Do not add any other colors.

Do another abstract piece, similar to the above, but use the opposite colors on the color wheel for the items you are abstracting from.

Furniture

Paint breakfast furniture. Use an old chair or table (not a nice antique), or buy unpainted wood furniture. Paint a breakfast motif on the furniture. It may be a scene, a pattern or a singular object that has to do with breakfast.

Add breakfast-related materials, such as jar lids, broken plates, utensils and packaging to make your breakfast furniture into functional assemblage pieces.

Table setting

Do the same as with the furniture above, except with breakfast plates, bowls, glasses and cups. Work in glass or ceramic. Be careful to use only glazes that are safe for making food-related items.

Do the same as above, but this time with place mats. Here, the material will be much more flexible, as you can use almost anything that can be wiped, rinsed or washed clean.

Sunrise

Paint or draw an egg yolk sunrise. Replace all or some of the scenery with breakfast items, but do so in a subtle way, so that it is not obvious to the viewer at first.

Paint or draw the early morning kitchen, with the low sun coming in through the window. Pay attention to the chiaroscuro effect of the raking light as it hits each object.

Create a piece in any medium honoring the sunrise. Interpret this any way you wish.

Fog

Depict a breakfast scene as viewed through the half-lidded fog of being not quite awake so early in the morning. This would, of course, be a semi-abstract work.

Depict one, two or three simple breakfast objects in a foggy, not-quite-awake still-life.

As more of a challenge, create a three-dimensional breakfast object in any medium, with the same half-asleep vision as above.

Rush hour

Do the same as in the Fog exercises above, but replace the hazy daze with the rush and zip of some modern breakfast scenes. Apply this sense of speed to one or more breakfast objects.

Paint a traffic jam, but in place of motorized vehicles, portray various breakfast items clogging the streets.

Lounging on the Sofa

Sofa elements – Couch, settee, day bed, long, soft, cushy, comfortable, fabric, slipcovers, pillows, bolsters, legs
Lounging concepts – Coziness, laziness, luxury, respite, sloth, comfort, relax, nap
Lounging on the sofa perspectives – Positions of self on the sofa, location of the sofa, the view from the sofa.
Lounging activities – Reading, petting the pet, watching television, listening to music, staring into space, drifting into sleep

Odalisque (sort of)

Portray a classic reclining figure on a sofa or settee. Include a significant amount of drapery in the background, and maybe also around the sofa. Make this a very romantic, dark and sultry scene.

Do the same as above, but have the color scheme be bright and light. Instead of so much drapery, depict a distant landscape that is receding into the background.

Think about possible sillier poses to replace the classic reclining figure.

If you cannot find a willing model, then use your pets, who will probably be very happy to nap on the sofa as they pose for you.

Sofa design

Design some kind of outrageous sofa, one that goes beyond the usual couch. Maybe it has more than one function, is covered in pockets, or has motorized wheels.

Design your dream sofa, based purely on aesthetics and comfort. Think about structure, frame, size, fabric, cushions and embellishments.

Draw fabric designs for a sofa. Consider color, pattern, texture and material. Come up with your own ideas or use one of the following themes:

- Buzzing insects
- Melons on the march

- Relentless heat wave
- Stripes gone wild
- Hometown highlights

Napping

Portray a scene from the point of view of how things look when you are freshly awake from a nap, when everything is still fairly hazy. How do things look from the sofa; the room, the floor, the ceiling, other people? Is everything spinning or just kind of foggy?

Paint or draw a scene, or create something that you saw, or sensed, while in the theta state. This would be the semi-conscious place between sleeping and being awake, while one is also somewhat aware of what is going on around them.

Do a portrait of someone freshly woken-up from a sofa snooze, with their nap-face, pillow creases, funny hair and rumpled clothes, and with their permission, of course. You can also do the same with a self-portrait.

Zoomorphic

Design, create or depict an animated or zoomorphic sofa. Maybe this sofa is a carnivorous plant swallowing the relaxee, or it could be horned and tailed, but sitting quietly. Create a sofa, a maquette, or portray someone lounging on, or interacting with, this sofa.

Create an installation piece of a whole room starring this magnificent beast of a sofa.

Boat

Think of the sofa as a boat in the living room sea, river, pond or lake. The sofa could either be docked or afloat. Paint or draw a nautical scene, a sweet and peaceful seascape with a regular sofa floating by.

Design a well-equipped sofa-boat with life-jacket pillows. If you were afloat in your living room and the waters were deep, what would you need on your sofa-boat? What would you like to have? How would the sofa be designed?

Daydreaming

Actual, real-live daydreaming is an excellent situation for emptying your head and seeing the sparks of inspiration that come. Drifting from lounging to a state of deep relaxation is wonderful for recharging the creative muscles. Daydreaming on the sofa is good for you.

Luxury

The simple luxury of having the time to lounge on the sofa is divine. See this simple luxury as extraordinary luxury and go opulent.

Design a luxurious, opulent sofa. Set it under a chandelier. Go nuts. Be extravagant. Be as outrageously lavish as you possibly can with your sofa design. There are no limits.

Imagine a worn-out and faded plaid sofa decked in velvet doilies and gold ribbons. Update your actual sofa, or adopt an old flea market find. Embellish the poor thing with luxuriant trims, tassels, beads and costume jewelry. Add anything you like to make it a lovable junkyard dog in a cashmere jacket with jewel buttons. Create a functional masterpiece.

Arguing

Arguing elements – Words, thoughts, ideas, points-of-view, reasoning, persuasion, disagreement, heated discussion
Arguing concepts – For the sake of argument, a difference of opinion, emotional heat, fighting

Words

Paint or draw a semi-abstract work based on the words of an argument. Have the piece be made of mostly actual written words and lettering. Think about the interpretation of the argument words and your color usage.

Create a three-dimensional piece that is also mostly made of the words of an argument being thrown about.

Do a double portrait of two figures juggling argument words separately and between each other.

Portraits

Do a head portrait of a single person in the middle of an argument. Have this person be arguing with someone off the canvas or paper. They may also be arguing with themselves.

Do a double head portrait of two people arguing with each other. Or they may be arguing with someone off the canvas or paper instead. Or maybe they are both arguing with the viewer.

Do a group portrait of people arguing with each other. Include at least one person arguing with someone off the viewing area. Any of these arguments being portrayed may be of the silent type.

Energy

Create a completely abstract piece depicting the physical and emotional energy of an argument. Do not use figures, objects, words or letters. As an extra challenge, do not use the color red.

Make a kinetic, possibly electric, sculptural piece featuring two inanimate objects arguing.

Points of view

Create a scene that depicts a few different sides of an argument at the same time. These differing points-of-view may be portrayed on opposing sides of the piece, or split into any number of panels, and may be intertwined.

Make a geometric sculptural piece showing three of more differing opinions, one for each side.

Housecleaning

Housecleaning elements – Soap, detergent, cleanser, sponges, scrubbies, rags, broom, mop, bucket

Housecleaning concepts – Purge, shine, scrub, wash, soak, sweep, clean, shiny, neat, sanitary

Sponges

Design a set of four cleaning sponges. Think about shape (anything but rectangular), color, pattern, motif and/or theme.

Use sponges as an art material. Create something using an assortment of cleaning sponges. Have the construction be at least 75% sponge. If you are stuck for ideas, do a quick free-write session on the subject of sponges.

Use sponges as a stamping tool for inks or other water-soluble media. Either use them as they are, which would be an assortment of rectangles, scrunch them up to make organic shapes or cut them into other shapes. You can also try cutting into the sponges to make a sort of high-relief sponge stamp.

String mops

String mops have personality, more than most other cleaning tools. Do a portrait of a string mop, either full figure or a headshot. Portray the mop as having even more personality than it may seem at first glance.

Create a scene involving string mops as the main characters. If you cannot think of a scenario, use one of the following themes:

- The 1978 Cleaning Disaster
- Mops on the Deep Blue Sea
- The Pumpkin Follies
- A Bucket for my Beau
- Any classic, historic or mythological scene that has been painted a number of times before, only this time with string mops as the leading characters

Scrubbing

Scrub a drawing or painting. If working in paint, use an old stubby brush, or a toothbrush, or a sponge. If working in graphite, charcoal or pastel, use an eraser or a stubby brush. Try anything as a tool to move your material around the paper, panel or canvas while using a scrubbing sort of motion.

Scrub a texture into what might ordinarily be a relatively flat surface. For the harder surfaces of some sculptural mediums try sandpaper, a wire brush or anything abrasive.

Make a mess

Make the ugliest, most miserable piece of so-called art that you possibly can. Just let yourself go. Purge intensively. Now, don't you feel better? You may now go and destroy this piece, throw it out, recycle it, stuff it in a closet. Remember, it's only going to get better from here.

I use a version of this exercise in my oil painting classes. I originally developed it as a composition tool. In any two-dimensional medium, make a mess on the paper or canvas. Make the nastiest, busiest abstract composition that you possibly can, the uglier and more cluttered, the better. Then stop and put the piece aside until at least the next day. Do not look at it. If you are working in oil, then let it dry for however many days it takes to dry, but again, ignore it as much as possible.

Continue with the last point. Look at the piece again. Take every compositional tool that you know of, refer to the list of visual elements earlier in this book, and clean it up. Paint over it, draw over it and/or erase some of it. If you are working in watercolor, you may have to switch to gouache, or you may draw over the piece in any medium. Do not cover everything from the earlier session, but work with what you have from before. Have at least 25% of your earlier session show through. Your goal is to make something aesthetically pleasing out of the previous mess. It can be done.

Actuality

You can always clean out your studio, rearrange things, scrub and polish your tools, and/or organize your supplies. Forget about making art for the day, but instead spend some quality time in your studio puttering around. Play some good music and put your studio back together. Sometimes just doing this will be inspiring.

Clean your art. Sand a few frames, re-varnish a painting, replace some mats, re-glue an assemblage piece, do whatever needs to be done to repair any damaged pieces.

Boredom

And if you are really bored or feeling the need to be challenged, untangle some yarn.

Shine

Do a representational painting or drawing focusing on portraying something shiny, glossy and/or metallic. Do not use metallic pigments or materials, but really examine what creates the effect of a shine. Portray just one shiny thing, so that it is the focus of the piece.

Do a representational painting or drawing of a multitude of actual shiny, glossy and/or metallic things. Have the composition be wild with perceived shine. Again, do not use metallic pigments or materials.

Do an abstract painting or drawing based on the shapes of shiny spots and highlights seen on actual items. Take these shiny shapes and make them into the major visual elements of an abstract composition. Use only a minimum of metallic pigments, no more than 15%.

Even shinier

Do what you usually do, but work even shinier. Try using metallic paints, pencils or inks. If you do assemblage or mixed-media, there are all kinds of materials you can add such as metal, wire, beads, glass, cellophane, etc. Add more of a polish or a sheen to your finishes. If you work in fiber, add some metallic thread or shiny fabric.

Create something with an internal light that emanates outward. Have the piece include three hues of the color red, an unusual texture, and at least six loops of any kind. It may also consist of anything else you like.

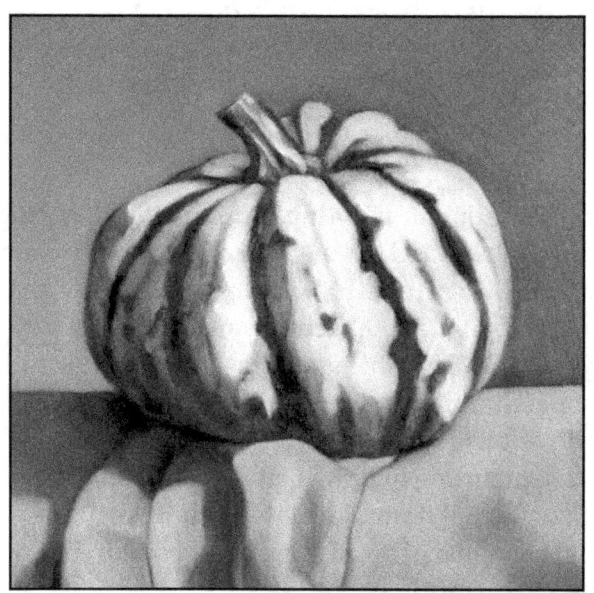

Finding Inspiration
in the Visual Elements

This chapter is about how to visually dissect the whole of what you see into its elemental parts, and then turning those observed visual elements into a source of inspiration. For example, you might see a branch of a tree. Looking closely at this branch you will also see the color of the leaves, the contrast between the bark and the sky, the lines created by twigs, and the cast shadows created by the light of the sun falling on the branch, and therefore that bit of light not reaching the ground.

This is a two-step process. First you search, find, look, observe and notice. Then you take what you have seen and create something else that is inspired by certain visual elements of the initial object, subject or scene. Some of these visual elements may be more conducive to creativity than others. However, observance of all of them will increase your perceptive abilities, and therefore your skill at being creative. So much of art is simply about seeing.

In this chapter I will be giving you more things to observe, although less specific things to do. You could try combining these observances with the exercises from previous chapters. Of course, you are always free to expand your mind on your own, to see where your thoughts might lead you to, as there is always so much more to explore.

Composition

Composition is the sum of the parts. It is about how and where the visual elements are placed or arranged to make a cohesive whole. Seeing composition involves some editing. Composition in life, as well as in art, is contained in some way. Inside, it is contained by walls, at the very least. Outside, it is contained by your peripheral vision at any given moment of observance. The composition of what you see may change in the next moment, but it will still be contained, no matter what.

In two-dimensional art the four-sided equiangular shape predominates. This would be the rectangle or the square. Why a four-sided shape with 90° corners? Is this a natural perception or one that we have been trained to think of in terms of vision? It's something to think about.

Composition is about editing. This would be signified by where either a form ends, or where the picture plane ends. You can use a window like a cropping tool to visually edit larger forms and/or to isolate them from distracting surroundings. This will work for anything that is viewed either in two or three dimensions, or anything that will be translated into a two or three-dimensional art form.

Take a regular piece of cardboard and cut a window into it. The cardboard should be about the size of notebook paper. Cut a rectangular window, about 3" x 5", into the middle of it. You would then have a nice frame around the window, about three inches all around. This will help you edit what you see. You do not want your vision to become cluttered. The window will help you focus on a composition. You can hold the cardboard at different distances from your eye to change the size of the composition you are viewing.

This cardboard window works like viewing something through a camera viewfinder. Place tracing paper over the window and trace what you see. Even better, get a piece of clear plexiglass, about the size of the cardboard. Use this to back your tracing paper, so that it will be easier to draw on. Masking tape will help hold the tracing paper in place. You now have a window-tracer for recording compositions that you see around you. You could take actual photographs, but this will allow you to concentrate on the composition itself and nothing else.

Take your window-tracer and find interesting compositions everywhere. Trace the placement of things by making outlines of what you see. You could start with small, two-dimensional things. Hold your window up to magazine pages and other pictures to make smaller, and possibly abstract, compositions. Try using your window on other flat things like older exterior walls where surfaces change frequently. This will force you to seek out interesting details in paint, brick color, cracks, texture and so on. Hold your window up to a view and trace the three-dimensional world. Shift the window ever so slightly. How does the composition change? View dozens of compositions. Trace only the ones that you find appealing. You can also make cardboard windows in other sizes. Try any of the following shapes for your cardboard window; square, circle, oval, trapezoid, triangle, and so on.

Simply by seeing all kinds of compositional possibilities, you may be inspired to set up your own visual arrangements in a new way. You can take the outlines or silhouettes you have traced and use them in an abstract composition.

Take a found composition as it is, but move one thing to change it, make it better, to give it some tension. Make a game of it. What one thing would you change to improve the composition? Would the tree look better on the other side of that door? Would that line be more interesting if it were tilted at a slightly different angle?

Another way to explore this subject is to use found objects instead of found composition. Look at what already is there on a table or desk, in a drawer, or in your pockets or purse. Do not add anything. Construct and arrange the things at hand into an interesting composition. Create a new way of seeing familiar objects, or concentrate only on their visual attributes. Be purposeful with the placement of your objects.

Color

Look at the amazing variety of color around you. Wow! We are so lucky. Color is such an extraordinary gift. It is such wonderful stuff. Shall I go on? Because I could, for pages and pages. Anyway...

Take a color by itself; a gorgeous color or an unusual color. Choose a singular color that you see on something around you, especially a color that you may not have paid attention to for awhile. You may also decide to use a dull color that you plan to make glow by virtue of how you use it and what other colors may be in proximity.

Create a piece of art where this color is the focal point; as a single hue or in a monochromatic range. Try using different percentages of your chosen color in relation to other colors, and see how you can have it stand out as both a small percentage and a large amount of the same color in different pieces of artwork.

A few examples of being having intent with an individual color:

- A stained-glass window, with the glass in a range of tints and shades of ultramarine blue
- A quilt sewn from fabric in a few close shades of rose-red
- An abstract painting that is at least 85% the color of orange juice
- A representational painting with the subject matter as seen through yellow-tinted glasses.
- A wood sculpture painted a certain shade of leaf green

There was a lunchtime game we played at art school sort-of called; 'How-would-you-mix-that-color'? We would choose a color from all of the things randomly sitting around us, and then each one of us would tell how we would mix that exact same color using oil paint pigments. This is a wonderful exercise for both understanding and really seeing individual colors.

To expand on this idea, choose two juxtaposed colors that you find. For example, I saw two overlapping flyers on public bulletin board; one was a deep teal and the other was a light orchid purple. These colors were lovely together. Finding a pair of colors is as simple as seeing a leaf and a petal on the same flower, or an old gray sock that had been unceremoniously dropped on a red brick sidewalk.

Look for interesting and/or unusual pairings of colors, either striking or subtle, that are not commonly found such as red and blue. Use any pair of colors that you find as a point of departure for a piece of art. For example, having been struck by the accidental pairing of teal and orchid, I could make a necklace using teal and light orchid glass beads. I could also make those beads myself using teal and orchid polymer clay. I could make a quilt predominantly in those colors, or a semi-abstracted painting of a tropical cityscape that is 75% in various shades of teal and orchid. Maybe I could do a small construction made of found and bought objects. I could go on a scavenger hunt in thrift shops and flea markets and see what materials I could find in teal and orchid. I could wear those two colors exclusively as I search for such things and have a friend photo-document the hunt.

The same sort of thing can be done with color schemes, or a range of colors. This is not to be confused with seeing massive amounts of color at once. You want the clear sense that what you are seeing has a certain color feel, which avoids the general visual clutter of what we usually see. Every now and then we will come across a place or view a scene that has a striking color ambience. This is usually more noticeable outdoors, and is much easier with nature. However, interiors can be included as well. Some examples of this are:

- The southwest desert after a rainstorm or during the hour before sunset; desert colors with a certain glow

- A rack of spring clothes (not the whole store) in a shop after a too-long winter; sweet colors that pop

- Autumn leaves, straw, pumpkins, gourds; the classic autumn color range

- A gray, overcast summer day, a white painted-brick house, black shutters and trim, with climbing ivy; black, white, shades of gray and glossy dark green

Notice a scene that has an interesting color scheme. Take note of five key colors. You might be at a party and see the coat pile on someone's bed. You notice a few black jackets, one cobalt blue parka and a bright magenta vintage coat. The bedspread peeking out from under the pile is a deep yellow and the walls of the bedroom are painted a medium shade of leaf green. There are your five colors; black, magenta, cobalt blue, deep yellow and leaf green.

Another day you might be taking a walk in town. You look in the storefront window of a bakery. There you see an assortment of cakes with white, pink and blue frosting. The cake trays are silver and the purple car parked out front is being reflected in the bakery window. Now you have white, pink, blue, silver and purple.

These are good, usable color schemes, but maybe you prefer something moodier. You continue walking, a late autumn wind blows in, and the sky becomes overcast as you stroll into a historic cemetery. You notice the graying of the sky, the various warm and cool grays of the headstones and monuments, the muted pale browns of the dying lawns, and the deep browns of the nearly bare branches of trees against the clouds. You also see a few bright red berries clinging to a bush that the birds have missed. And speaking of birds, you notice a few crows over there in the trees. You now have grays, straw brown, dark brown, black and a few dots of berry red.

In the last few days you have collected three five-color schemes. Use any one of them as the focal point for a piece of art. You may do a color abstraction, focus your material usage with only these five colors, or set up a realist tableaux using the same set of colors to reflect the ambience of what you saw. You may do a color-expanded version of any of the earlier suggested exercises or ideas. Let color itself be your inspiration.

Contrast

Contrast is signified by comparing the visual relationship between two separate things in proximity, or two planes of color and/or light on the same thing. The point of contrast is seen along the edge that separates one thing, or plane, from another.

There are two basic types of visual contrast. One is between shades of dark and light, such as the chiaroscuro effect. The other is between different colors. There is also the degree of contrast. High contrast is when the difference is striking. Low contrast is when the difference is barely noticeable.

Light and dark contrast is best displayed by stark black and white, such as the keys on a piano or on the fur of a black cat with white paws. A cardboard box in strong light will also show high contrast with one side in a warm shade of light brown, and the shadow side a dark cool brown. The edge between the two sides will display the strong contrast. You can see a high dark/light contrast with a tree branch that is backlit by a bright sunny sky. A low degree of dark/light contrast can be seen between most things in a dimly lit room or outdoors at dusk, for example. A gray squirrel sitting on a weathered backyard deck will be of a low dark/light contrast.

Color contrast, on the other hand, could be of similar dark/light tones. However, the colors themselves are what designate the line of contrast, where two very distinct colors touch and share an edge. Orange and orange-red would be a low color contrast. Orange and blue would be a high color contrast, even though they both might be of the same comparative value of gray. The most striking contrasts would be where there is both color and dark/light differentiation. Think of a four-square equation. The four quadrants of the square are high color contrast, low color contrast, high light/dark contrast and low light/dark contrast. All visual contrasts fall somewhere in the larger box, inside one quadrant and near or far from another, depending on the level and type of contrast.

In the visual arts, contrast can also be considered in texture, material and/or surface, all of which may be signified by either color or dark/light contrast as well. For example, in a mixed-media piece you might show contrast between velveteen and aluminum. Even if both materials are the exact same color and shade of silver-gray, there will be contrast. That contrast will be seen by the visual cues that the texture of the materials give; by how light hits them, in the reflections on the surface of the metal, and in the minute shadows on the surface of the velveteen made by the threads of the fabric.

Experiment with high and low contrasts in color, degree of light and dark, and in surface texture. Do contrasting studies of similar subjects. Some ideas for this are:

Do paintings or drawings of fruit on a plate, in any style. High contrast could be lemon wedges on a deep purple plate. Low contrast could be oranges on a red-orange plate, or honeydew slices on a pale green plate. Or even better, do the same lemon wedges on the purple plate as before, and then on the pale green plate.

Do a pair of representational paintings or drawings of fabric in strong directional light. For one, use a piece of draped white fabric, for the other use dark gray fabric. Doing this will give you a wonderful lesson in light and shadow. You may also portray both pieces of fabric in the same drawing or painting. Drape the fabric so that there are at least a few interesting folds in each piece.

Create a mixed-media piece. Make sure that all your materials are in similar shades of at least four distinct colors. For example, you may use an ash brown wood frame, turquoise-blue stained glass scraps, old copper tubing and green acrylic paint. Or you may decide to use green, red and blue acrylic paint on a small piece of copper sheeting bordered with twigs. The contrast will not be in light and dark, but between some of the colors. Each color will contrast against at least one other color, but if you were to take a black and white photograph of the piece, you would see mostly similar shades of gray.

Sew a quilt completely in similar shades of any one color, but include pieces of different fabrics with a wide range of textures such as velvet, cotton twill, satin, corduroy, felt and burlap. Trim the edges with matching buttons, shiny ribbons and pompoms.

Light

Light is the illumination that allows us to see the world around us. Light emanates from a source, or a reflection of that source. Sources of light are the sun, fire, lightning and various types of light bulbs. Minimal sources of light would be stars (for us here on earth), fireflies and phosphorescence. Moonlight is an example of reflected light. There is also ambient daylight, such as when the sun is not shining directly on something, the sky is overcast, or even when the sun has already set, but there is still visible light outside.

Any light source will have a major effect on your work, whether it is being created or being viewed. The direction in which the light source originates is especially important. The degree and direction of light will affect highlights, shadows, reflected light in shadow, reflection of any kind, and color. The position of the sun is static. It is the earth that moves, but since we cannot control the spinning of the earth, we must be aware of our physical relationship to the sun at any given time of day or year. We have more control over illumination coming from light bulbs and candles, and we can create shadows by the careful placement of other objects.

Pay attention to your sources of light. Note where it originates, how many sources there are and if reflection is involved. Is ambient daylight a factor? How can you change or adjust your light sources to affect the way your artwork appears? Do you need to move your finished piece, or your working set-up to get a different visual effect in regards to light? Move yourself, and therefore your viewpoint and see if anything changes. The word light is also often used in reference to the tint of a color, or a pale hue, such as when people say in regards to the noon sky, "it is light blue". Light is a value of a color, a tint of a deeper color. For example, when enough white paint is mixed with dark green paint, you get light green paint. Sometimes a light color is produced by a strong direct light falling on an object that is a medium tone. This would create a highlight, which is lighter in color than the local color of that item.

Sitting where you are right now, see how may highlights you notice on each object around you. By being conscious of light you will become more aware of all kinds of visual cues. Carefully replicating the abstract shapes of highlights, for example, will bring you closer to working representationally.

Try painting something simple with either an overhead ceiling light or any other kind of general ambient lighting. Then paint the exact same thing in the same position and lighting as before. However, this time add a small spot lamp aimed directly at one side of your subject to create strong lights and shadows. See the difference?

Take any object with simple coloring, carry it around, and see how the colors change according to the available light in different locations.

You can also use any light source as your subject matter. This can be a wonderful challenge, depending on how you define the word light. Consider the definitions I have mentioned here, and think of any I may have forgotten. You can combine definitions in your piece such as reflected light, light colors and tiny light bulbs on strings. You can also use light as a material, or as the theme or concept for your artwork. Of course, be cautious of playing with fire and electricity. Use common sense and non-flammable materials.

Shadow

Shadow is defined by the side of something that light does not fall upon. For example, one side of a tomato sitting on a windowsill is illuminated by the sun, but the side of the tomato that is facing away from the sun is in shadow. The shadow side of anything will always be darker in color than the illuminated side. Shadow can also be a cast shadow, which is sometimes known as shade. Your own shadow on the sidewalk is a cast shadow, made by your figure blocking the light that falls upon your body from the other direction.

Shadow shapes are the shapes of the shadows. Easy. But shadows have more depth to them besides being simply dark shapes that fall upon the ground. These shapes do not always mimic the objects that interrupt light flow. They can be quite distorted, depending on how they fall. Their edges can be sharp or fuzzy, they can be high or low contrast in relation to the illuminated areas around them, and they can hold reflected light within them. In fact, they usually do. Look hard at a shadow. See how the edges are darker than the area within? The lighter area inside a shadow is reflected light. Sometimes other colors are reflected in there too. Shadows are also transparent things, even if they fall on opaque objects.

Start paying attention to shadows. They are fascinating worlds unto themselves. See how the great masters portrayed shadows. Try using one of their methods in your own medium. Do tracings of cast shadows to come up with interesting shapes. Use your small piece of plexiglass and tracing paper.

Apply these abstract shapes to another project. Use shadow, with any of its possible definitions and physical realities as your subject matter. If you don't know where to start, do a free-writing session beginning with the word shadow.

Mass

Mass is the larger areas of light or shadow on a subject or scene. Mass is not an individual shadow, or a spot of light, and really has minimal relation to individual objects. It is the larger shadow shape that may fall across part of a shoulder, arm, abdomen, leg, corner of the chair, part of the robe and ends in a patch on the floorboards. A light or shadow mass crosses edges and boundaries between things to make a larger shape unto itself. You need good directional lighting to have strong masses in a picture.

When I first learned about the concept of massing, I began to notice it on television a lot, maybe because of the strong direct studio lighting. Observing mass (in the religion of art) is wonderful practice. You begin to see it everywhere. Working with the concept of mass is excellent for achieving visual realism, because it redirects the larger picture of what you see into its abstract parts.

Look at anything and separate the light and dark areas. This is massing. This idea works especially well on visually fluid and organic things, such a people, draped fabric, mountain ranges (although not at high noon when the sun is directly overhead) and plants.

So, what can you do with observed mass purely as a visual element unto itself? I dunno. See, even this absurdly creative girl gets creative blocks. It happens to all of us.

Of course, the above definition applies mainly to the visual properties of the two-dimensional world. There is also physical mass, which is the full shape of a three-dimensional form. This is another thing all together. I think it could be very interesting to take the form of one thing, say a fish and apply it to another, such as flowers. Then you could have a bouquet of blooms molded into the form of a fish, or fish forms growing from the ground like flowers or budding from trees. You could take the form of a fire hydrant and interpret it as a train to come up with all kinds of ideas. For example, you could create a train made of horizontal hydrant cars running on a water track, or maybe you could paint fire hydrant forms as an engine, a coal car, a caboose or a double decker sleeper car. Look at any form that you find intriguing, and apply the mass of the three-dimensional shape to something else that is completely different.

Line

Some people say line doesn't occur in nature, but in my opinion, that's a lie. Some people also say that pure black doesn't occur naturally either, and that is wrong as well.

Line is wonderful stuff, and can be quite beautiful on its own. Line is visual poetry. Line is musical. You will find both actual and implied line in such things as edges, borders, creases, twigs, string, paneling, corduroy, stripes, kitty whiskers, leaf veins, markings on shells, and cracks in the wall.

Sitting where you are, list twenty or more different lines that you see around you. Describe these lines according to the various qualities mentioned in the chapter about the visual elements earlier in this book.

Make an abstract or semi-abstract piece, either in two or three dimensions, using a minimum of four of the line qualities from your list of twenty types of lines and not much else. Drawing or painting lines can be easily done. For sculptural works, you can use wire, sticks, yarn, cord, glass rods, coils, or any other linear material. You can also cut paper, fabric and other things into lines that you can use for your linear piece.

Think about the direction of a straight line. Choose a scene, or set up a still-life, with 80 to 90% of the lines going in one direction, and the remainder all going in another. Or do an abstraction based on directional lines that you have observed.

Create another piece; pictorial, abstract or anything in-between, using only fluid, curved, curly, zig-zag types of lines. If you need to, limit yourself to no more than three main colors for the piece. First make up a fun title like "The Zig-Zag Epoch of the Firefly Days" or "Boomerang Bustier". Then you can make the piece fit the title, which could be more of an interesting challenge.

Edge

An edge is where one thing ends and another begins, including open space. An edge can also be the very thin side of something, like the edge of a piece of paper. In artwork, edges are where the physical mass, or two-dimensional plane, of a piece of art ends.

Edges in artwork can be intriguing places. A lot can happen on or near the edge, both aesthetically and in terms of meaning. What you decide to place there can be of great importance. When you go out to look at others' artwork, pay attention to how the edges are treated. Would you change anything?

Pay attention to the edges in everything you see, including the edges within things where there might be a change in color or texture. Look at the side edges of things, as well. Notice the nature of the edge. Is it sharp, smooth, fuzzy, or blended into the next thing? How is the level of contrast? Consider the implied edge of something, or the edge as an imaginary line, such as a crease. What is the quality of that line/edge?

Do a two-dimensional piece, in any style, with most of the subject, action and/or color on or near the edge of the piece, but not much going on in the middle. Base this idea on something that you see around you, or that you have observed recently. For more of a challenge, try this exercise in three dimensions.

Bring the idea of the visual edge into the center of a piece of artwork, using line, color, texture or another element. This might be like turning something halfway inside out, or could be as simple as bringing exterior lines inward.

Are your edges edgy? Are they so cutting edge that you need a sharp pair of scissors? Do useless terms like these annoy you? Play with the meaning of the word edge. Create an actual cutting edge of something. Consider portraying a real edge, like a cliff.

Balance

Visual balance is how you see two or more things in relation to one another. By creating artwork you are framing these objects and/or elements within a confined space. It is in this process of framing, and therefore editing, that you decide on the visual equilibrium of the piece. This is usually not done by mathematical formula, but is more of an aesthetic sense based on a personal comfort level.

Play with the ideas of balance, off-balance and out-of-balance in two-dimensional art. Move something around. Adjust, tweak or change your viewpoint. Consider the center, and all of the options involved with something being off-center.

You can also balance actual things, both visually and with actual weight. Inventing scales and other systems of balance can be a fun thing to try if you are three-dimensionally inclined.

Symmetry in Balance

Lateral symmetry involves a center line, either visible or not. Everything on one side of that line is replicated in exact proportion on the other side. We are designed by lateral symmetry, with our spine being the center line. Other examples of lateral symmetry would be a bivalve shell, a violin or a butterfly. Look for things around you that have lateral symmetry.

Take any object or scene. Hold a mirror up at any point within the object's edges. This will give you a split-image. The point where the mirror meets the object is now the center line, and what you see is now lateral symmetry. You can create artwork using these images; either exactly as seen, or straying from them as much you like.

Radial symmetry emanates evenly from a center point. Examples of radial symmetry are sunflowers, pentagrams and targets. Look for things that have radial symmetry.

You can invent radial symmetry. Take something and look at it through a kaleidoscope. You can also base anything you see on the idea of radial symmetry. Take elements from your pet dog, for example, and have them radiate from a center point. Maybe place the dog's nose in the center. You can then have rings of eyes, tongues, paws and tails all radiating in layers to create a sort of daisy-dog.

Horizon Lines in Balance

The horizon is where the earth meets the sky, and it also is where the table meets the wall. Look for all kinds of horizon lines; on the earth, in skyline silhouettes, where a figure in repose ends and the drapery behind him or her begins to be visible.

Think about the placement of the horizon line on the picture plane. Depending on the composition, it will look good anywhere but dead center. However, at some point do a landscape with a dead-center horizon line, just because.

Draw a horizontal line on any kind of paper, and then draw a scene on a separate piece of tracing paper. Move the tracing paper scene over the static horizon line to see how the picture is affected by its position.

Try painting or drawing a few similar scenes, but each with a very different horizon line.

Using a scene that you know well, raise or lower the skyline to your liking.

Take a few different existing horizon lines, and some other scenes that you are familiar with, and then mix and match the skylines with the scenery to create hybrid landscapes. For example; you have a desert scene, a beachfront boardwalk scene and a big city skyline. Now portray the desert flora in front of the skyscrapers, the boardwalk eateries and souvenir shops in front of the desert mesas, and the city traffic and street-life in front of the ocean horizon.

Consider the skyline silhouette as an abstract shape, and create a three-dimensional form based on it.

Odds and Evens in Balance

Even numbers are divisible by two. Odd numbers are not. Simple as that. Look for groupings of things, whether they are like objects or somewhat dissimilar items. Just look and count the number of things you see as a visual group under any definition. Use your cardboard frame to make quick compositions of little scenes that you see around you. How many main objects are there? Is it an odd or an even number?

Odd numbers are generally considered more aesthetically pleasing, but even numbers can work just as well in a composition if well positioned.

Try setting up different arrangements of things. Do a drawing or painting of three objects, and then four of the same object. It could be as simple as three apples, and then four apples. Do you see the difference, besides the actual number of main objects? The three apples will fall into a pleasing composition much more easily than the four apples will. However, four apples can make for an interesting picture, depending on how they are positioned.

Combine odds and evens in one piece of artwork. If you see three oranges on the kitchen counter, and there are four glasses on the table, use both sets of things in a still-life. If you are abstract-inclined, use three ovals and four triangles in the same composition.

Edges in Balance

Use your cardboard window and look at a rectangular piece of the world. See if the composition is visually weighted to one side. Maybe an object or visual element goes off one edge and out of the picture plane. Think about what you can do, add, subtract or adjust to another side or edge of the composition to balance the whole thing. You are not looking for symmetry, but a more captivating sense of balance.

Tension

Tension can create an intriguing balance in a composition. It describes a sense of 'pull'. it is a visual minor key, a barely-just-there dissonance. If the composition were completely dissonant, however, there would be no tension.

Take any composition and pull one element all the way over to the edge so that it is almost off-balance, but not quite.

Use your cardboard window and look for compositions with a sense of tension. Find that place between balance and off-balance. Shift things in one direction, ever so slightly, until you find it.

Portray something that is on the verge of falling or is being pulled. Have the composition reflect that sensation. Think about how the use of color reflects the idea of tension. Have your color scheme be not quite easy, but still have a sense of harmony within it.

Pattern

A pattern is a surface print on something such as fabric, wallpaper, gift wrap, animals (leopards, Dalmatian dogs, zebras), mottled leaves, and some shells and rocks. Patterns can be made by groupings of similar things such as piles of eggplants in the produce market, fish in a wishing pond, flower gardens, brick walls, shingles and fences. A solid color is not a pattern, and neither is a gradient.

Patterns are usually even, symmetrical and/or repetitive. They are the visual experience of something that is covering the surface of something else. Patterns are not any old various mix of different things found in the same general area. There is some quality of repetition to a pattern, either regular or random.

As said earlier, a printed pattern can be made of design elements, pictorial icons, random marks or geometric shapes. There are also "naturally" occurring patterns such as crops in a field, among other things mentioned above. Look into a pond and see a school of fish. They become a fish pattern. A cloudy sky gives off a cloud pattern. You will see a leaf pattern in a healthy summer hedge. An unhealthy hedge, or a winter hedge, will display a twig pattern. These can all be seen as surface patterns by framing what you see in your cardboard window.

Look for both printed and naturally occurring patterns around you. Use one or more of these patterns as a background for a still-life or a portrait. A real challenge would be to paint or draw a piece of draped, patterned fabric as part of your composition.

Use a pattern of any kind as the basis for an abstract piece of art. Match the colors of your pattern sample, and then change the original design as much or little as you like to achieve some level of abstraction. For example, take a piece of flower-printed fabric. Now view these same printed flowers as though you were rushing by, you have just woken up and everything is blurry, or you have been spinning and came to quick stop, as the corner of your eye caught the piece of fabric. How does it look at that moment?

Portray or build something that is not naturally patterned, and then give it a pattern, or change the pattern of something that already has one. For example, a house cat's fur can be portrayed as having the pattern of actual tiger stripes, or maybe its fur is in a colorful cartoon dog pattern. A pumpkin can be covered with a Halloween candy pattern, or a pattern of pictorial plumbing parts if you feel like being random. Maybe you prefer to cover the pumpkin in dark purple and light blue checks.

You can work with the placement of actual objects to create a three-dimensional pattern for either an installation or assemblage piece. Use items with some visual similarity, or that have a meaningful relationship with one another. Or you may decide to be as random as possible, and make a real-life object pattern out of a grouping of things such as buttons, orange peels, old telephone cords and glasses of water. Let the audience have some fun figuring out what it all really means.

Create your own non-objective patterned objects out of clay, yarn, wood, bottle caps or any other sculptural material. Make a bas-relief or assemblage pattern using constructed or sculpted shape-objects. A few examples would be a geometric grid of wooden cones, a visually random pattern of coils and mounds in clay, or a mosaic made of tiny stained-glass triangles and round buttons.

Repetition

Visual repetition is when something you see re-occurs over and over again. It often refers to a pattern or a row of something. Some examples of repetitive things are stripes, polka dots, fence posts, telephone poles on a lonesome highway, a long row of glasses sitting on a shelf in a bar, cereal boxes lined up on display at the grocery store, windmills on a wind farm and rows of crops in a field.

Look for visually repetitive things as you go through your day. Any of the ideas and exercises given for visual patterns can be applied to the idea of repetition. You can also take a singular something and repeat it over and over again in a regular sort of way.

Mirrors are a wonderful tool for playing with the concept and visual actuality of repetition. Think about when you are sitting to get your hair cut, and your head seems to repeat forever.

Perspective

Perspective relates to the position in which you are viewing something, and then how that something recedes into the distance. The further things are from your viewpoint, the smaller they get. A tall person in the distance will appear to be tiny in comparison to the young child standing right in front of you.

The easiest way to demonstrate this is to look at buildings, because they are usually geometric in form. Use your plexiglass tracer and look down a street. Trace the flat tops of the buildings. Even though they may go at different angles, you will see that they are all striving to reach the same point on the horizon. You may not be able to see the actual vanishing point on the street, but the lines of the rooftops will lead you there. This is perspective in action.

Move a few steps away and look at the changed perspective of the same scene. Step onto a platform and see how the perspective changes. Look straight up at a tall building (be careful) to get an interesting take on perspective. This viewpoint often gives one the sense of falling backward.

Look at a box or a straight-back wooden chair to see perspective on another scale. Observe an item from different angles, as well as from above and below. Can you find the vanishing point in an enclosed room, or could it possibly be somewhere outside the room where you can't see it?

Trace a set of perspective angles and lines from anything you see. Then take these lines and apply them to something else. Force the perspective of a tall building onto a still-life of fruit, for example. This would be a sort of artificial exaggeration of one thing based on the parameters of the other thing.

Skew the perspective of something else. Maybe you could have a nice red barn with the vanishing point being up above instead of way in the distance.

Path

The path is a visual concept that gives the person viewing a piece of art a road for their eye to travel. Ideally, this road leads the viewer to see the whole piece. While looking at a painting, pay attention to where your eye goes first. What do you look at next? Does your vision follow a path? Is there a place for your eye to rest?

The places that initially attract the eye are human or animal faces, clock faces, the color yellow, light or bright colors on a dark field, and other points of sharp contrast. Do you see any of these particular things when you first look at a work of art? Any number of visual elements can by used as a means of creating an entry point and a path in a piece of artwork. Among these are color, contrast, edges, line, triangles and faces.

Close your eyes, and then open your eyes. What is the first thing you notice in the room in which you are now sitting? What do you see next? Take note of the things that draw your eye to look around the whole room. What are the elements that guide you on this path?

Collect path elements that you have actually seen. During a walk outdoors you might notice a bright yellow sign, an orange traffic cone, a number of faces, a garden hose, and a hedge along a sidewalk going off in one direction. Use these items purposefully in a made-up composition that emphasizes the idea of the path.

You can use some of these found path elements in a non-path-like way. Arrange them in a disconnected anti-sequence, or maybe have them be all on one side of your composition. See if you can use visual path elements in a way that does not lead the eye around. And then, what do you need to add or subtract to re-create the path so that the viewer's eye can travel the whole piece of artwork?

Triangles

Triangles are three-sided, three-angled enclosed shapes, with all sides being straight lines. Triangles are a classic form of composition, and can create a visual path. Like paths, triangles can be implied by the use of color, contrast, edges and line. A triangle can be the large triangular shape of the main subject or object, or a triangle shape made by a few main objects that are overlapping each other. They can also be represented by three similar objects or colors placed on a triangular path, that can lead the eye around the piece of art. In a two-dimensional composition you might see three distinct areas of a light yellow-green color; a slice of lime in one corner, a chartreuse silk scarf on another side and a branch of new spring buds out the window near the top. Or you might see three sources of light being portrayed; a light bulb, a lit candle and the crescent moon. In an abstract piece you might see two patches of red, and then another spot of orange-red in a composition that is mostly made of cooler colors.

Any kind of triangle will do, depending on the individual piece; equilateral, isosceles, scalene, acute, equiangular, obtuse or right triangle. A tiny little triangle alone in one corner will not cut it when it comes to shaping a compositional path; neither will any form of triangulation that is located completely over to one side. It must cover the composition to the extent that the eye is enticed to travel the course of the picture plane.

Using your cardboard window take note of the triangles that you see, whether by complete shape or by trios of objects that are visually alike. Move your window around until you can see all kinds of triangles. Use one or more sets of the triangles that you have observed in a new composition of your own.

Do an abstract piece based on actual triangles and trios that you have seen.

Use triangular shaped objects or forms in a three-dimensional piece.

Portray a single object, subject or color three times as triangle angle-points in a two-dimensional composition. Do another one where the same three items are placed in new locations on the picture plane, to make a different sort of triangle.

Arrange a figure into a large triangular shape, or combine a few overlapping figures for the same effect.

Form

Form defines the physical space that something occupies. It is the three-dimensional shape of a physical being, object or group of objects. Because it is three-dimensional, it can be sensed by touch as well as sight. Walk around a form and look at it from different angles. Touch the form if you are allowed (see texture below). Impress what you feel into memory.

Look at the two-dimensional outlines of three-dimensional things. Trace those outlines using your plexiglass tracer. Fill in the outlines to make a silhouette. You'll get some wild shapes and some plain ones too, depending on the angle of your view. Many of these shapes will not even resemble the original object. All outlines and silhouettes can be used as the basis for abstract two-dimensional work.

The form and shape of almost anything can be used as a design element unto itself or as an embellishment for other things. For example, think of shell or leaf shapes as ideas for repetitive patterns, or their forms as inspiration for an abstract sculptural piece. A high-relief beaded wall piece could have a design based on the delicate forms of twigs and branches with early spring buds. Maybe you could design a walk-through installation piece based on the many forms of icicles hanging from the deepest months of winter.

The form of one thing can also be transformed into the form of something else. Take anything you see and portray a second item using the form of the first object. Create a series of sculptural birds based on the forms of fruits and vegetables. Design a small fleet of boats inspired by the shapes of lizards and other reptiles.

Texture

Texture can be signified by vision, and therefore be a visual element, through a mix of personal experience, past knowledge and the play of light as it falls on an object and creates shadows. When you combine what you observe with what you might already know about the particular surface of an item, then you can safely guess at its texture.

Touch is the sense that is associated most often with the element of texture. Texture is signified by how the surface of something feels to the touch. Plants, fabric, shoes, produce, furniture, architecture; all these things and more offer many kinds of textures to experience.

Make note of textures that you find interesting to the eye or pleasing to the touch. Then, in a different medium, replicate it. Carve something furry out of stone. Paint or draw something especially slimy, and try to replicate that sensation in paint, pastel or charcoal. Knit a gravelly scarf in honor of your favorite country road. Stitch a dotted line down the middle.

Take a texture and exaggerate it. You can apply this to anything. If something is only slightly ridged, then make those ridges extra deep. If you have cotton candy texture, then make it especially light and airy.

Use the texture of one thing that you see and apply it to something else that you also see. You might take the velveteen from a sofa pillow and decide to apply it to the coffee mug, thereby making a velveteen mug. You look at the base of a lamp and then your cat walks into the room, so you decide to create a wrought iron kitty.

You could also make an abstract piece in any medium that is all about texture. Start with the textures you see around you. Create either a construction or a depiction of multiple textures.

Material

As the word is used here, material refers to the art supplies or other items used to create an individual piece of artwork. Material can be visually noted by seeing its texture, and understood from your own previous knowledge. When you look at artwork; especially assemblage, mixed-media and installation art, take note of the materials used. Look for unusual usage of materials, as well as artwork created from interesting things.

Visit stores that sell all kinds of potential art materials such as fabric, yarn and craft stores, hardware and lumber stores, hobby stores, plastic supply stores, any kind of miscellaneous parts stores and of course, art supply stores. See which of these raw materials inspire you, especially if they are not anything close to your usual medium.

Use new, different or unusual materials for what you normally create in the studio. Add something new to what you do. Or design a different framing or presentation treatment for your artwork.

Use an odd and/or contradictory material when you create something. For example, make something normally hard and tough out of soft fabric or fiber, such as a television made with dyed chicken feathers. If you find an intriguing new material, think about what you could create that would raise entertaining questions about the finished piece.

Make a piece of artwork, or a series, that is all about the material. Do paintings or drawings depicting materials, such as a series of portraits of skeins of yarn. If you work in three dimensions, create something that enhances the character and/or meaning of the material that you are using.

Size, Space and Volume

Size, space and volume can involve actual measurements, general proportion, or the relative size of something. Distance and perspective can affect the visual measurement of things. Eyeballing, or guessing by eye, can be a way of estimating the position of something in relation to something else. Volume can be the space that an object takes up, or it could also refer to the internal volume of a container.

Holding your cardboard window at various distances from your eye will show you how an object can take up different amounts of volume in the space of a composition.

Look at similar things in different sizes such as ostrich and chicken eggs, daisies and sunflowers, or lemons and pomelos. Play with distorting proportion in your artwork and see if any meanings shift, since size can mean importance, prominence or age. Think about the concepts of trial size and economy size.

Warp the sense of space between things. Consider such ideas as spaciousness and density, and how these ideas might affect volume in a composition. Look into contained volume, how much or little can be stuffed into a vessel of any kind, and what that could possibly mean.

Finding Inspiration
in Music and Sound

The Power of Sound

Sound is powerful stuff. Even though most of us learn about the world more through sight than any other sense, sound permeates our world. You can close your eyes, but not your ears. You can turn away from looking at something, but you cannot turn your ears away from hearing a sound. It is much easier to listen to the radio while working on something else, but not have the TV on nearby. The picture on the television is more distracting, and you must look away from your work to give it your full attention. A radio stays put, demanding no such thing.

The idea of entertainment, which encompasses much of music, is significantly more powerful than the visual arts are in our culture. Imagine there being televised awards shows for visual artists. Imagine the video equivalent of a radio sitting on the bureau, beaming non-commercial images of fine art for three minutes each. And hey, if one of you invents an artio, I want credit, royalties and airplay. Well okay, there is the internet, but I'm talking about an appliance made exclusively for viewing broadcasted fine art. Not programmed, but broadcasted.

I listen to music when I paint, and I often sing during the process. It's hard to dance while creating artwork, unless of course you are an action painter. I personally think that performance art is, ummm, a performing art, like drama, music and dance, and therefore I do not consider it visual art. There is some wonderful performance art out there, but in my opinion it is a form of theater, not visual art.

Seeing Sound

There is a condition called synesthesia, of which I have written more in the next chapter on language. Synesthesia concerns the natural synthesis, or combining, of different senses. It is how some of us are wired, so to speak. The most common form of synesthesia involves letters and numbers having colors. Less common forms involve sound, smell, taste and touch. Hearing a certain sound may stimulate a certain smell or color to a particular person. For example, a certain musical note, such as E, may spark the smell of roses, while the musical note D incites the smell of rotten eggs to the exact same person. Different notes, different smells.

For someone else with synesthesia, the sound of each musical instrument may have its own color. That color never changes. The sound of violin will always be purple, for example, whether that music is orchestral or bluegrass. All that matters is that the sound of violin equals purple. For another synesthete with the same instrument/color crossover, when he or she hears a violin, the color yellow comes to mind, instead of purple. These are not conscious decisions. They are just natural visual (or other sense) qualities that automatically relate to the original sensual (meaning; of the senses) catalyst.

If you are a synesthete, then the ability to see sound will most likely come easily for you. For the general population, certain sounds have color connotations according to meaning. For example; sirens equal red, and ocean waves equal teal, aqua and white. But as with anything, how one person may visually perceive a certain sound will most likely be different from the next person. And that's okay. Each one of us sees a little differently in the mind's eye. Beauty is in the eye of the beholder and all that. So is how we perceive things. The natural diversity of individual taste is affected by perception, and this results in a wide variety of artistic expression. Different people will see the sound of a chicken scratching around the yard differently from each other.

Sound travels through time. Sound waves travel through space as well, but there is a time element to sound, even on the scientific level. We perceive sound as having a beginning and an end in terms of time, from when you first begin to hear it, to when you can't hear it anymore. A bus goes by, but for you the sound of the motor begins and ends when you first start to hear it until you don't hear it anymore. For this chapter we will deal solely with perception, and not whether a bus in the forest makes a sound if there are no passengers.

For the purposes of visual interpretation, sound either has a beginning and an end, or it can be cropped to do so. A sound can be edited to fit, let's say, three minutes. Now you have this three minute line of time that goes from left to right (as an example). Next, you have your parameters of audible sound from high to low. You now have a two-dimensional space to visually fill with the sound you hear, going left to right, up and down. It's kind of like sheet music, only a lot more visually expressive and less mathematical.

Begin exploring this idea on a simple level. Do a simple drawing to start. Work left to right. Higher pitched noise sounds go towards the top, lower vibrations below. Depict the quality of the sound; whether it is full, tinny, screechy, flowing, rhythmic or any combination thereof. Space things left to right according to rhythm and sound intervals. Take any sound you choose and describe it in one word or more, and then illustrate that sound-word. Make marks, lines, splotches, blend colors, have sharp contrast. If the sound is full or complex, then make layers of marks, lines, colors and masses. Does the music or sound have a sense of tension? See what I wrote about the visual element of tension in the last chapter.

Next, you can explore working in any direction; right to left, down to up, diagonally or radiating from the center.

Much of what you do at this stage will be abstract. However, all ideas that begin as abstractions can be useful for representational work, which relies on the basic elements of composition, numbers of things, line and rhythm. For depicting music, add tone. Something that starts out as a pure abstract interpretation of sound can be used as a blueprint for the placement of items and the color scheme, as well as the type of background given to a representational piece of art.

Where Sound Can Be Found

Anywhere! Just listen, slow down, pay attention and dissect what you hear. Separate out the sounds from the general cacophony of life. For example, right now in this room I hear a pen scratching on paper, a ticking clock, a few birds twittering, cars accelerating and braking, an airplane buzzing overhead and trains pulling into the station.

Consider the sounds that you hear. Cars sometimes have a peeling sound. Think of peeling apples and the peels falling to the table or floor. Depict the concept of peeling. The bus snorts to a stop. It's a big old bull discharging passengers. I've often thought of buses as bees, going from stop to stop like bees to flowers. The bus is now a snorting bull-bee, hungry for people-pollen. The upstairs neighbor walks to another room and the floor creaks. This house almost sways in the wind, it is so ramshackle. Does the floor creak like bedsprings? Does the house bump and bobble around? Would it get up and leave if it could?

All you need to do is to pay attention and listen. Take it one sound at a time.

Ambient Sound and Vibration

All sound is created of vibrations. Low vibrations are slower, and therefore are deeper in sound. You can often hear the distinct vibrations in bass of any kind, whether it is from a guitar, a cello, a low voice or the deepest keys all the way to the left on the piano. Faster vibrations create higher pitched sounds. They create a smoother sound too, since there is less space between the sound waves. A carefully stroked violin string creates a continuous tone of sound. Think of photography. Slow vibrations in their lower pitch are grainy.

Ambient sound is general background noise. White noise is the roar of constant traffic, motors, air conditioners in the summertime, and also the sound of large crowds, as well as waterfalls. It is a continuous sound that is always there. Nothing in particular stands out, but sometimes there is a faint ebb and flow in pitch and volume.

There is a truck that has been idling outside for quite awhile now, giving off a low rumbling growl. It is a snoring bear, a hibernating semi. I see this sound as an all-over abstracted pattern of vibrations, ripples in a small range of assorted dull colors.

I grew up in Queens, New York. In the summertime our sixth floor apartment windows would be wide open to catch any possible breeze. I clearly remember the constant roar of the countless air conditioners humming away on sultry evenings. I now see/hear them as a hollow, muddy water, tunnel-like sound. I see greenish-brown and transparent dirty aqua colors as I hear them, with a little grayish-white thrown into the mix.

If you are fortunate to be near a waterfall, listen to the rushing quality of the sound. It is dramatic and soothing at the same time. Do an abstraction based on the sound of the continuous roar of falling water. Forget what a waterfall looks like. You are illustrating only the sound. Later, if you decide to do a realist painting or drawing of the waterfall, combine what you now understand about the sound with your approach to the piece. Your waterfall landscape will be much stronger for it.

Think about the connection between the sound that you hear and the visual properties of the thing giving off that sound. The big, solid, box-like truck and the low, grumbly purring emanating from it. A silky, streaming mass of flowing water juxtaposed with the impatient roar.

Do an all-over constant abstract design piece, like a mottled color field, according to the qualities of any ambient sound that you choose. Hear a constant type of sound and illustrate it exactly as it is, with all its audible peaks and valleys. Make a series of consistent marks all over, like a scrap of low-pile carpet.

Contain background noise. Use the visual pattern of any ambient sound as the literal background to a portrait or a still-life. Try doing a series of different things, each one portrayed using the visual interpretation of its own individual sound.

Word-sounds

Buzz, crackle, hiss, roar, squeak, squeal, swoosh, tap, thud, thump, tick tock, whoosh, zoom. Ah, the raw sound of nothing in particular. It is defined by the quality of the sound itself, and not necessarily by what makes that sound.

Use any of these words, or other such sound-words, in your artwork to help illustrate the description of the sound itself. In other words, include the words.

If you include words in your artwork, you can then use the visual properties of the sound to embellish the word itself. Or make the whole piece about the word, and not much else.

Paint, draw or create something that makes that word-sound using the visual quality of that sound. For example, a portrait of an old, rickety rocking chair that obviously squeaks a lot when in use, painted with the visual qualities of the word squeak. Use squeaky brushstrokes, squeaky line and squeaky colors. Define that visual quality of squeak for yourself.

Do a pure abstraction on how you think any particular word-sound looks and feels.

Human Speech

Of course, when we speak, we make sound. Singing is human speech as music. Somewhere in between is poetry, soliloquy and drama. Listen to the sounds of individual words, and the poetry of full sentences. There is rhythm and melody in the chains of spoken words. Listen for the spaces between the links.

Also consider the sound quality of the human voice. There are many descriptive words here; sweet, gravelly, high, low, drawl, speedy, shaky, nasal, squeaky, goofy, thin, full. All of these words have visual connotations, as well.

Take a sentence that someone has spoken, or record yourself, and make a visual translation of it. Use the simple method in the section on seeing sound. Break the sentence into rhythm and melody. Use marks, lines, masses and color to make a simple abstracted guide to the way that sentences are spoken.

Portray the quality of the sound of someone's voice, or do a vocal self-portrait. Depict what you hear by paying close attention to color, edges and texture.

Listen to a spoken-word poem. Even better, record yourself reading your own poem. This way it will be totally yours, completely original, and you will avoid any copyright issues. Paint, draw or re-create the poem using some, or possibly all, of the words in the visual cadence of the rhythm of the spoken poem.

Take a single word and portray it as an abstraction using pure feeling, expressed visually. Do not include the word in your piece.

Animal Talk

Songbirds, crows, seagulls, woodpeckers, ducks, barking dogs, purring cats, cows, sheep, other farm animals, bees, flies, cicadas, mosquitoes and squirrels. They all have wings to beat or something to say. Even a buzzing insect has something to tell you by virtue of its flight and proximity.

Portray an animal by using the visual qualities of the sound that it makes. For example, a buzzing bee painted in the vibrations of the buzz. Bonus points for not using yellow and black.

Do a completely abstract piece, or a series, based on the raw sound of any animal.

Mix and match. Paint or draw a duck scene using the visual qualities of the sound of barking dogs. If the sound is harsh, cluttered and loud, use quick and assured marks going in a number of different directions at once. Use the colors red, blue and brown. The ducks may be scattered about, some of them might be upside-down. Of course, you may interpret the sound of dogs barking differently than I have mentioned here. Just for you, a few other mix and match ideas:

- Portray a moose using the visual qualities of the sound of excited seagulls at the beach

- Create a farm scene inspired by the sounds of various buzzing insects

- Paint or draw a group of scampering squirrels with the visual sound of honking geese

Street Noise

Lawn mowers, leaf blowers, jackhammers, helicopters, buses, cars, idling trucks, honking taxicabs, wailing sirens, and trains click-click-clacking on tracks. And that's just in the first twenty minutes.

Invent descriptive words for how any of these noises sound. Then create a cityscape using these new words. For example, bdm-bdm-bdm-bdm and pheeeeeuuuw. Take these two new words and incorporate them into a city scene, with the letters as buildings, vehicles and so on.

Create an abstract street scene completely from your visual interpretation of the noise you hear on the street. Instead of a building being made of brick, its surface would be a sound-pattern reflective of what is heard on the street.

Listen to construction or street repair noise. There's all kinds of interesting sounds echoing in here. I'm listening to some right now. They're tearing something or other up around the corner. There are hums and rhythms and screeches, all waiting to be translated into something visual. Do a sculpture or installation piece based on the sound of street construction.

Particular Sounds

The sound of glass breaking, bells clanging, fire crackling in a fireplace, eggs frying, rain on the roof, a babbling brook, the radiator hissing, ocean waves lapping, audience clapping, restaurant conversation and the ringing, ringing, ringing of the telephone.

Illustrate a scene by the quality of its related sound. For example; an audience that is portrayed in the staccato rhythm of the sound of clapping, or a telephone still-life re-created in the high-pitched loopy curl of the sound of its ringing.

Do an abstracted piece based on an actual something that includes both the quality of its visual sound and a 10% to 20% recognition factor of the object or subject itself.

Free-write about something and its sound. Then pull sound-word-images from your writing. For example:

Babbling brook, a lumpy, curly flow. Babbling babbling softly churning burbling lipping lapping at pebbly rocks, a giggling gurgling turning and twisting liquid flow as it goes on its way with tiny pearls of spray.

Then you can do any of the following things:

- An abstract piece based on any or all of these wonderful sound images
- A landscape that includes a brook, enhanced by the visual sounds of a babbling brook
- A piece about a babbling brook that is actually babbling real spoken words, to itself and anyone else who will listen

Seeing Music

Songs and other musical compositions travel through time. They can be measured from beginning to end, and they almost always are when recorded. To start visually interpreting music, use the same approach from the section on seeing sound from earlier in this chapter. Do something simple at first to begin exploring this idea, and then you can make things more complex and expressive as the music moves you.

Do songs have colors? If you are not a synesthete, then you can think about what color typically means, such as oranges are hot and blue is cool. Tropical music may be represented by tropical colors, and Celtic and Irish music would mostly be in a range of greens. Early punk would be black, gray and hot pink.

Think about the notes, the space between notes, the chords and the beats. Consider all the different qualities of music. Make a mark, or a series of marks, according to where in time the sounds fall, the places they occupy in the composition. You may come up with a thin, linear piece or a full, rich, layered brocade of visual musical sound. This is about turning a musical composition into a visual composition.

There must be at least a thousand different categories of music with all their periods and hybrids and cultural influences. I almost subjected you to a list of them, but that would take pages. You can go to a record store or look at an online music site to get a feel for the diversity of musical expression this world has to offer.

Like art, music is a living tradition. This means that creative and cultural expressions evolve from that which has come before. It is not static or completely unchanging. Hybrids develop when two or more living musical traditions come together and influence each other, like Afro-Cuban music or Punkabilly.

I once did a painting called Peculiar Music, a melancholic industrial landscape influenced partially by the sounds of Bulgarian Choir music. I appreciate the strange math found in interesting music, and I think in similar ways when mapping out my own visual compositions. My paintings, in a way, are snippets of my own visual songs.

Rhythm

Rhythm is beat, as expressed by time signature. Three quarter time, or 3/4, would be three actual beats played in the space of four beats, with one of the four being silent. Either that, or I am terribly wrong. Go ask one of your musician friends. Knowing time signatures can open up all kinds of compositional ideas for rhythmic artwork. Rhythm is also affected by speed, which is expressed in wonderful sounding Italian words such as "staccato" and "pianissimo". Time signature and speed of playing can be visually interpreted as marks and intervals.

Think about the rhythm and/or speed of a piece of visual art. How speedy or rhythmic it feels to look at can be seen by clutter, proportion, and clarity of path.

Do an abstraction based on the rhythmic beats and intervals of a piece of music.

Use any rhythm you choose as the basis for the placement of still-life objects on a shelf or trees in a landscape.

Arrange similar objects according to different time signatures to create an installation piece. As a very simple example, place a row of cones in 2/4 time, a row of blocks in 3/4 time and a row of bottle caps in 7/8 time.

Remember that rhythm can be visually expressed in directions other than horizontally left to right. Rhythm can be vertical, diagonal, shooting out like stars, or displayed in an all-over pattern. Try interpreting the same rhythm from five different angles.

Melody and Harmony

Melody is expressed by a series of notes, and by the individual character of those notes, such as duration. A song's melody is also its tune. Musical notes fall on a scale. The western scale of music is based on twelve notes, seven of which are A, B, C, D, E, F and G. In between are flats and sharps, which make up the other five notes. There are other musical scales and systems, such as in Eastern music. Talk to your musician friends. They'll tell you more. Melody can be seen as lines, strokes, even flowing forms and movement. Melody is the consecutive arrangement of musical notes. This line is the path that a tune will take. Harmony is a second (or third or more) layer of melody. Harmonies add dimension to melodies. These layers can overlap or not.

Interpret a melody as a two or three-dimensional line in a piece of artwork.

Add layers of visual harmony as multiple lines or a mass.

Portray a melody as a path, either in two dimensions, or as an actual path that is a site-specific installation.

Create a harmonic piece in ribbons and other linear materials.

Notes, Keys, Chords

These elements are the color of music. Each key has its own feel to it. Minor keys have a sadness, a sense of melancholy, a darkness to them. Major keys are more upbeat (regardless of any actual beat). A particular style or genre of music will also affect the emotional quality of the piece.

I would imagine that each musical key has a corresponding color. If each note had its own color, then a key might be a color range, and a chord would be a set of three or four colors. Or each chord, by virtue of its own combined sound, may have its own color, or even a multi-color shimmer.

Decide which colors go with each musical note, key and chord. Develop a system with a corresponding chart or map. If you are a synesthete, use your actual vision of these things. If not, then apply the color you feel suits the particular tone, or set of tones, the best.

Using one bar of music from any song you choose, create an abstract piece using only the colors corresponding to the notes in that bar. This will also work well with choosing a color scheme for a piece of fiber art.

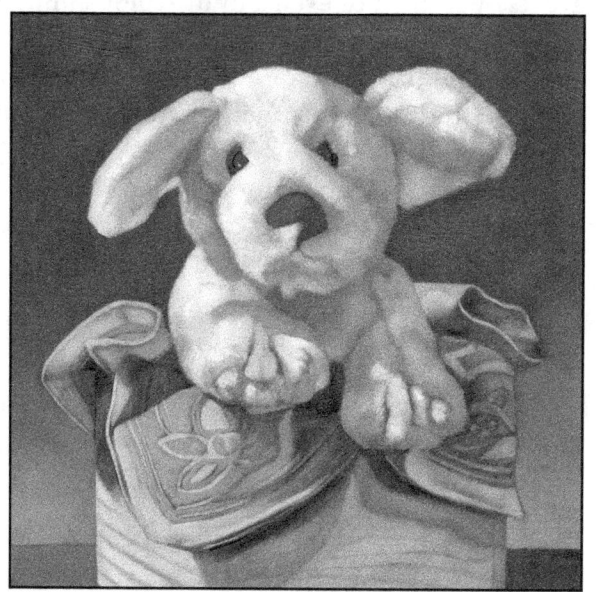

Finding Inspiration in Language

Synesthesia

For as long as I can remember, each letter of the alphabet has had a corresponding color. So do numbers, days of the week and months of the year. Each one has their own specific color, or color shimmer where a certain letter may fluctuate in the space between two colors. For example; 2 is butter yellow, T is black and Wednesday is a warm tomato color such as cadmium red light. I think of a number or look at a letter, and I automatically see the color. This was not anything I ever questioned. I always though it was normal, and it is normal for me.

A few years back I read a letter in a magazine that mentioned this word, "synesthesia". There was now a name for this phenomenon for me. It is when senses get crossed. For example, the sense of sound is stimulated, and someone with synesthesia not only hears the sound, but also sees a shape. They may hear a piano being played, but they are also aware of the shape of a rhomboid while listening. It's just there for them.

Only some people have synesthesia, a small percentage of the population. Many creative people do. Don't despair or feel less creative if you don't. If you don't have the preconceived notion that the letter F is blue and the numeral 8 is brown, then you are more free, and it will be easier for you, to portray them in other colors as you choose.

Synesthetes (people who have synesthesia) don't consciously assign colors, smells, shapes or anything else to other things. These odd descriptive qualities for things are inherent, meaning they are a normal property of that other something as perceived by that one particular person. We each have our own individual systems for perceiving certain things. My letter R may be a deep red, but for another synesthete, the letter R is a pale cool green. Neither of us is right or wrong. It's purely individual perception.

Make an alphabet chart with each letter portrayed in its own color. If you have synesthesia, use the colors you already see. If not, or for synesthetes who want a challenge, then you can assign colors according to any system you choose.

Do the same thing as above with numbers, geometric shapes, names of states, or any other system you would like to categorize by color.

Free-writing

See the earlier chapter on the process of free-writing for some background. Below is one process for finding inspiration from self-written poetry:

1. Take any word, or short phrase, from something you are seeing, doing, thinking or reading.

2. Do a short free-writing session based on that word or phrase.

3. Make a poem, lyric or ditty out of it.

4. Cull word-images from the lines you have written.

5. Create artwork that you have interpreted from the word-images.

6. Bonus! You have a poem! How multi-talented you are!

Here is an example of how this process works:

1. You are eating an apple.

2. *Eat an apple crunchy meat see it oxidize inside outside upside down twirl on a stem while counting to ten, so shiny red and green tiger-striped inside it seems to be turning brown golden creamy pale yellow and shadow green eat an apple eat it down a cliff on the edge of the top of the thing for a tiny little being big drifts and ski slopes and bites taking shape and a line on the rim of the skin.*

3. *Eating an apple*
   with its pale yellow meat
   all crunchy and sweet
   twirl on a stem
   so shiny and red
   and tiger-striped green
   see it oxidize
   inside outside
   upside-down

   Eat an apple
   while counting to ten
   eat the thing down
   a cliff on the edge
   of the golden interior
   now turning brown
   watch it oxidize
   inside outside
   upside-down

4. Three examples of word-images from this free-write poem:

- twirl on a stem
- tiger-striped green
- a cliff on the edge of the golden interior

5. Some ideas and visions for creating artwork interpreted from these three lines:

Twirl on a stem

The first thing I see is tiny ballerinas dancing on apple stems. Then it could be anybody twirling on any kind of stem. Or maybe it is the stems that are twirling. This evolves into the idea of twirling on its own; the dizzying, winding motion of twirling. Consider the various types of stems from fruit to pumpkins to brains. There are countless creative ideas that can be realized from any of this. What comes to your mind from what I have written so far? Imagine what you will discover with your own free-writing and poem-lyric-ditty.

Tiger-striped green

First, I see a green and black striped tiger, then a green and orange tiger. Then I consider greenery that is tiger-striped, or maybe a striped putting green. Green can mean innocent, as in unripe. Tigers are tough, so I think tiger-striped green could mean innocently tough. Forget meaning, shift back to color. Imagine different colors for the usual things. Besides green tigers, this could translate into blue hearts, orange clouds and silver darkness.

A cliff on the edge of the golden interior

There is a cliffscape with golden yellow soil instead of the usual red, brown or black. Of course, if you've spent time in the desert or anywhere volcanic, the soil is all of these colors and more. However, I am currently living in an area with brown soil, for whenever we are lucky enough to see any soil at all. But enough of this dirt... Maybe there is an almost real skinned-apple cliff exactly as I saw it after taking a bite. Or the apple, or the cliff in question, both are real gold in the interior, with all the possible meanings; the cliff, the precipice, the harrowing edge of a golden interior.

6. Bonus. You also have something to read or sing to your kids, your neighbors' kids, or to all the sweet pets that you know.

Where to Find the Written Word

Words can be found almost everywhere. Whether this is convenient or annoying depends on the situation. For these circumstances, we will decide it is convenient. Trying to paint a plein air landscape with a billboard blocking half the view, well, I would call that annoying, to say the least. Unless, of course, you like the billboard exactly where it is as part of the composition. Anyway...

The written word can be found on those very billboards, neon signs, storefront graphics, the sides of buses, down in the subway station, in skywriting, on cereal boxes, covering your junk mail, on various tags and labels, and all printed matter for that matter. You can also find an abundance of words on TV, all over the internet, and during movie titles and credits.

Can't decide on a word to be your source of inspiration for a project? There is always the dictionary. Close your eyes, flip through the pages, settle on one by feel, and point until your finger hits the book. Open your eyes and there is your word. Use this word as a point of departure. If you don't like the definition, then use your first reaction to that word. See what picture comes to mind immediately upon reading the word.

Think about the idea of written words being everywhere. Cover your whole artwork with various words, without regard to meaning.

Have your artwork be about one word, using that actual written word in the piece as well, but in a subtle way. Consider the meaning of your word. Choose colors accordingly.

Have an abundance of words be your subject matter. Fill the background atmosphere of your subject matter with words; either spacious, cluttered or solid with words. Maybe there are so many words that it all becomes just one big word. Create an installation or a sculptural piece about how the air is filled with words.

The Sound of Words

Consider the sound of individual words. Are they soft and flowing? Are they harsh and sharp? Are they rough and bumpy? Also consider the sound of spoken phrases, exclamations and questions. See the previous chapter on sound for more on this subject.

The Visual Style of Writing

Think of various styles of writing such as elegant calligraphy, early hip-hop graffiti on New York City subway cars, late 1960s psychedelic posters and early punk band flyers. Notice all the various fonts in printed matter and on screen. There are thousands of different types of type from formal script to chunky block, and everything in-between. Research font libraries. Some are very entertaining. Notice individual letters and numbers, and whole alphabets, and how any of them might be presented to make a certain style.

Seek out different styles of writing. Try imitating them, or create your own version. Make art posters based on your new writing style, or your interpretation of a classic genre, such as wedding calligraphy or street signage.

If you can't think of something, then invent your own writing style based on any of the following concepts:

- The vegetable garden
- Waiting forever for the train
- Dreamland
- Weather or not
- Old sneakers

Study any style of calligraphy. Play with chiseled markers and pens with different nibs. Get serious. Have fun.

Paint words using interesting materials and tools such as sponges, sticks and old toothbrushes.

Design a completely new font. If you don't feel like designing a whole alphabet, take one letter and design ten different styles for that letter.

Take a word in a plain font and artistically embellish the word. Take a word in a fancy style of writing and simplify it, smoothing out the edges.

The Shape of Words

Write a word, or enlarge a printed word in any font, and trace the shape. Use this shape as the basis for a sculptural form. Repeat a series of this shape for an installation. Use the two-dimensional shape in a drawing or painting. Cut printmaking paper to this shape before printing.

Build or draw a shape. Fill in the shape with a word, a phrase or a sentence.

Tags and Labels

Create tags for specific things out of non-cloth materials such as glass or grapefruit peels.

Cover something that you make with tags, including fabric tags.

Collect actual tags from anything. Create something from all these tags.

Tag your art. Write instructions, either real or arbitrary.

Consider the instructional tag. Create an assemblage piece that is all about the instructions. Make up random instructions or write a conceptual statement with hidden meanings.

Design a series of tags without words. They may be blank, color-coded or include pictorial symbols.

Think about the idea of labels. Create sticker labels. Label things around your house, or use removable labels in public places. Make it curious.

Hybrid Words

In this case, hybrid words are any two words joined together with a hyphen to make a new word. One example would be scarf-dog. This could be a dog that always wears a scarf, a dog that scarfs food down (like most dogs), or a scarf that is the companion pet of another scarf. Take any two things you see, any two actions going on nearby, or any sensation or exclamation you randomly choose. Mix nouns, verbs, adjectives or any other classifications of words together.

If you cannot think of any hybrids off the top of your head, begin with any of these examples:

- box-stripe
- pillow-fish
- drawer-blue
- carpet-phone
- sky-lime
- table-hey!

Create something in any medium or style based on your interpretation of any of the above hybrid words.

Do a split-comparison piece, where half is about the scarf and the other half is about the dog. This is actually quite a common approach used by artists, usually to make some kind of a statement. Think about any meaning you might wish to convey, or if it is purely about random thought.

Make a truly hybrid piece of art, not only inspired by a hybrid word, but hybrid also by mixing your use of materials, approaches and/or artistic styles. For example, sky-lime could be a mixed-media piece mounted on a small board. The sky could be painted realistically with blue and clouds, and the lime could be an abstract in different shades of green glitter and sequins. Sky could be on the left and lime on the right side of the board, or the lime could be placed in front of the sky. The lime could also be portrayed on the front of the piece, with the sky on the back. Maybe the sky could be made of fabric pieces glued to a large wooden lime. The possibilities are many.

Make a chain of hybrid words such as: snorkel-spoon, spoon-mouse, mouse-tomato, tomato-pond. You can loop the chain with pond-snorkel, if you like. With these hybrid words you can create an intertwined series of pieces, like an accordion fold book or a giant domino set. Brainstorm, and see what ideas come.

If you know any other languages you can make interlingual hybrids. Although not fluent, I have a moderate working knowledge of Spanish and a tiny little bit (un pequeñito) of Japanese. The first thing that comes to me is tako-taco, which can be translated into octopus-heel. Okay, silly example, but you get the idea. Both are beautiful and fluid languages, and although grammatically quite different, they are similar in pronunciation. So, what can you make of octopus-heel?

Learn Another Language

There are great benefits to knowing another language. Even with speaking and understanding a small amount, you get the opportunity to see the world through the eyes of different cultures. Languages evolve around different needs and experiences. You will be exposed to verbs and adjectives that have no equivalent in English. This opens up new ways of seeing things, which is always helpful for expanding creativity. New languages (new to you) involve new visual sounds, pronunciations, phrases, colors, twists of grammar, and fresh meanings for all the usual things. At the very least, look through a few phrase books for travelers. Whole worlds will open up for you.

Random Words in Art

The use of written language is fairly common in modern and contemporary art. Many of us have played with the concept of mixing words and visual images at one time or another. Words are usually incorporated into artwork to enhance the meaning of the piece.

Try adding words that are completely unrelated to the pictorial images you have chosen. For example, imagine an image of a pineapple with the word brick written across the bottom, a soft sculpture of a blender with a tag that says alligator, or an unpainted wooden form with the words blue, green, and purple carved into the side.

Color Poem

Using your own synesthesia colors or your assigned color chart, write a poem letter by letter, color by color.

Assign a color for each whole word in the poem, based on your own color-feel for each word.

Choose a color scheme (a few colors or a range of colors) for a whole poem. Base the colors on your interpretation of the feel and/or subject matter of the poem. Think about of your style of writing. Consider having the writing or font style reflect the sense of the poem, as well.

Forget the words of the poem as written letters. Instead, use small color blocks in any shape, with each color representing a specific letter, as in your synesthesia color chart. Think of this as writing your poem in a secret code.

Solitary Letters

Take a letter, maybe one of your initials. If your initial is Z, you can do a painting of the letter Z, a drawing or a series of prints. You can go out in the world and photograph the letter Z wherever you see it. You can sculpt the letter Z, and you can make a letter Z out of anything you like, even caviar and diamonds.

Create a solitary letter using materials that have something to do with the letter, such as the letter P made entirely of pinecone parts.

Draw or paint something inside a letter shape that also reflects the letter, such as the letter M. You could have a mountain scene, a portrait of someone whose name begins with M, a bunch of other abstracted Ms that are all tangled up, or you could visually translate the sound of Mmmmm.

You can do the contrary thing. Take the letter S and fill it with illustrations of things that begin with the letter G.

Finding Inspiration in Life Events

Moving to a New City

Moving elements and concepts – Change, journey, a new chapter in life, moving forward, saying goodbye, the fear and thrill of the unknown; boxes and other packing materials; packing, physically moving stuff, stairs, trucks, unpacking, setting up a new space; maps, exploring, acclimating to the new place; paperwork, research, notifying people; new street address, numbers; the concept of cities, suburbs, countryside, roads, landmarks, regional differences and familiarity

Boxes

Decorate the outside of corrugated moving boxes. Paint scenes of moving on their sides. Embellish them with moving paraphernalia, such as designs made from masking tape and bubble wrap trim. Give them wheels, so they can move themselves. Using a thick permanent marker, write hints and clues all over them for what may be packed inside.

Create boxes out of anything. As an extra challenge, use flexible materials such as fabric, leaves or cellophane.

Use old boxes in an installation piece about the process of moving.

Make a castle from used corrugated moving boxes.

Packing materials

Think of packing materials as another source of art supplies. Create something out of any of the following:

- Bubble wrap comes in different sizes and even a few rare colors, plus, it makes that delightful popping sound
- Clean newsprint
- Tape, which comes in all kinds of colors, widths and textures

The grand puzzle

The logistical puzzle of packing and moving is very intensive.

Create a three-dimensional puzzle based on placing a mixture of odd-shaped items into a square or rectangular cube. The objects must fit tightly, so that they will not rattle around in transit.

Do an abstract piece based on scheduling logistics. Think about changing all your personal and household accounts, forwarding numbers and addresses, notifying everybody, moving yourself, your family and your stuff, cleaning out the old place and settling into the new one, and the careful timing of everything.

Redecorating

Rearrange your room. Just start moving stuff around. Look at your room in a whole new way.

Paint your furniture (not the good stuff). Paint stripes, geometric designs according to the lines of the piece, or maybe even landscapes or interior scenes. Paint a few pieces of old furniture; each one a slightly different solid color.

Repaint your walls. Paint or collage a mural. Do your ceiling.

Turn a room, or your whole home, into an installation piece, with each room having a theme.

Maps

Design a map of the route that you took to move. Illustrate the map with actual or symbolic landmarks. Choose particular marks, lines and masses of color to depict your thoughts and emotions about the move.

Collect road maps from flea markets, thrift stores, yard sales or your closet. Use the maps in a collage. You can even make a full installation piece out of them, if you have enough maps.

The journey

Create an illustrated road journal, an artist book telling the story of your move, either literally or figuratively. You can do this as a scroll or an accordion panel book, as well.

Design a board game based on the geographic journey of your own life. Do a free-writing session to get you thinking about the concept and guidelines of the game. You will need to design the board, player pieces, cards, etc. Think about what you need to do to win the game and what it means to win.

Create a series of small two or three-dimensional pieces symbolizing each place that you've lived. As a series, be aware of both the similarities and differences of each place-piece.

Memory

When you leave a place, you will be committing the parts of your former everyday life to memory. Unless, of course, you know someone who is still living there. In that case, you can sit on the old toilet again.

Paint or draw interior scenes of your old home from memory.

If you didn't like the place much, then portray it as a horror house.

Depict or construct your former home as seen through the mists of time. Exaggerate this passage of time, so that a place you left three years ago is seen as being antiquated.

Floor plans

Make a floor plan for your dream house and/or art studio. Hold nothing back. Create exactly what you want.

Draw or paint how this house and/or studio looks from the outside. Do the same for interior views. If you work in three-dimensions, then build a scale model.

Bulk

Portray bulk and weight. Do an abstraction depicting the weight of the things being moved. Use heavy colors, lines and forms. Consider thick materials.

As a challenge, do the above using lightweight materials, lines, forms and colors.

Create a kinetic piece involving the idea of physically moving heavy objects.

Too much stuff!

Make something out of everything you have that you could do without, such as yard sale leftovers.

Create an assemblage or installation from things you packed and moved, but are now wondering why. Add text to the piece.

Adopting a Pet

Pet adoption elements and concepts – Animals such as dog, cat, fish, reptile, pig, rat, ferret; new pets with old pets, the idea of a companion animal, a mascot for your life; odd pets, inanimate pets, cages, pet toys, food bowls, bedding, pet outfits, matching pet outfits; showing your pet its new home, caring for your pet, unconditional love, being inspired by the singular beauty and grace of your pet

Portraiture

The portraits listed below can be done in any style or medium.

- Do a portrait of your pet, or of others' pets that you know and love.
- Do a portrait of yourself with your pet.
- Portray yourself as a pet, either yours or someone else's.
- Do a double, triple or quadruple portrait of new pets with old pets. Include the ideas of love, friendship, competition and jealousy between particular pets.

Unusual pets

Depict or create odd pets that are actual animals, or creatures. Portray them as a typical dog, cat, bird or fish with all the usual accessories. For example, imagine a pet vulture in a fish bowl with a plastic castle and colored pebbles. If you need ideas, here are a few more:

- A pet octopus playing with a ball of yarn
- A pet bear on a swing in a birdcage
- A pet caterpillar with a rawhide bone in its mouth, wagging its tail

Consider inanimate objects as pets, such as a tomato pincushion. Portray it wearing a leash, while sitting near a fire hydrant. Here are a few other ideas you can use:

- A bottle of spray cleaner with a harness and bit around its nozzle, wearing a saddle while out in the pasture

- An old shoe sunning itself on the windowsill, with a catnip mouse by its side

- A grapefruit sporting a rhinestone collar

Make a mascot

Create an imaginary pet or mascot for a chapter in the story of your life. For example, think of having a rhinoceros as a sidekick for a time when you needed some extra strength, power, oomph. Depict or create this rhinoceros in any style that fits its meaning, and consider your material usage as well. If your rhino is powerful, yet thoughtful of delicate things, use strong, but seemingly fragile materials. If you needed to fend off enemies, real or imagined, at the time, then give the rhino extra horns and spikes.

Comic books

A wonderful source of two-dimensional inspiration for visual artists is the comic book store. Quite a bit of the work being printed in comic book format, sometimes known as the graphic novel, is brilliant. Many of these artist-illustrators are masters at combining their drawing skills with keen imagination and original storytelling. Like anywhere else, being exposed to others' good work can spark your own creativity.

Draw scenes of you and your pet in comic book format. Illustrate real or imagined adventures. Begin with one panel, then add a few more and work up to doing a whole comic book.

Put together a fanzine for your pet. Include photographs, interviews, letters, graphics, and anything else you can think of as a tribute to your dearest companion.

Design a movie-type poster glorifying your beloved pet. Use only black, white and any two colors.

You can do any of the above in collage, assemblage or artist book format as well, if you're feeling more tactile and/or three-dimensional.

Accessories

Go to any pet store, and you will see they are not just selling pet food. Household pets need accessories. Not a lot, but some. Below is a list of pet accessories that you can design and/or create. You can make actual useful things or more fanciful versions that will never be used. Create purely for aesthetics and/or for function, depending on the pet.

- Food and water bowls
- Pet toys
- Bedding
- Collars and leashes
- Cages and crates
- Cat structures for climbing

Welcoming your new pet

Write and illustrate your new pet's guide to its new home. Use a significant amount of pictures, since most of them can't read. In this guidebook, show them where everything of importance to them is located, and how to use things. Let them know what they should avoid. Include a schedule for mealtimes and walks. Illustrate all playtime options.

Design and/or construct a dream pet habitat, cage, closet, enclosed porch or whole room.

Create love notes for your new pet, like childhood Valentines and such. See the section on Falling in Love later in this chapter for more ideas.

Outfits

Do a portrait of your pet as an archetype or another animal. For example, do a painting of your dog in a duck outfit or dressed as the goddess Diana or Artemis.

Design or create pet outfits for different weather, for formal occasions, as costumes or disguises, or to fit your pet's alter ego. Be aware that your pet may or may not want to wear anything besides their own fur, feathers, scales or fins. Some pets are cool with dressing up, others will have no part of it. Respect their wishes.

Design or create matching outfits for you and your pet.

Losing or Leaving a Job

Job loss elements and concepts – Pink slip, getting the boot, downsized, walking out, filling a box with your stuff; the feeling of loss and panic, financial issues, pressure; closing one door so that another may open, free time, decompression, relief, change; identity, job title, label

The job from hell

Depict scenes from the job you hated most. Why was it so awful? Portray such awfulness in an awful way.

Create a chart of symbols representing aspects of why you hated your old job. Look at standard universal symbols and note how they portray meaning in a simple and direct way.

Choreograph the walking out dance. Although this is written for the visual arts, and is not a book about performance, I'll make an exception here. Plan the perfect exit. Design costumes, scenery and the script for your dream quitting scene.

Pink slip

Design and/or create a real pink slip that can be worn for the occasion. Is it elegant for going out in style, or bizarre for leaving them guessing, or is it seriously uncomfortable and ill-fitting for an unhappy exit?

Design and/or create something involving the abstract concept of the pink slip (maybe like a banana peel, only pink). Think about other meanings of the words pink and slip.

Get a bunch of used slips from the thrift store and dye them pink. Create an installation piece based on all these pink slips.

Do an abstraction based on the sound of the words pink and slip (just about now, the word slip is losing its meaning and becoming very strange to me). Do one piece that is about 90% in different shades of pink, another that is equal parts pink and one other color, and as a challenge, one with absolutely no pink at all.

Downsized

Do a portrait of yourself as being very small in a large space.

Do a series of increasing smaller self-portraits.

Do a series of things becoming increasingly smaller in any two or three-dimensional medium.

Loss, rejection, panic, falling apart

Portray a realistic scene of what actually happened when you lost a job, including any of the above-mentioned emotions.

Depict your feelings of loss or panic in a purely abstract way, with no representational objects depicted at all.

Think about the push and pull of rejection that results from being let go from a job that you wanted to leave anyway. Express these mixed emotions in a hybrid of styles and/or materials.

Create a two or three-dimensional portrait of yourself as literally falling apart in pieces. Then do a similar portrait of yourself as reconstructed with bandages, rubber bands and/or tape.

Create scenes of anything falling apart and/or being put back together.

Decompression

Depict relief, comfort and a general lack of stress in a realistic scene or in a purely abstract way.

Create or depict the idea of decompression. Think of an accordion expanding, or of anything that has been held tight against its will finally being let go.

Design and/or create new types of clocks and systems for the strange concept of unscheduled time. How does the clock function differently between having and not having a job?

Closing and opening doors

Create a system of doors whereby closing just one, another door automatically opens.

See the section in the Urban World chapter on using windows as a source of inspiration. Translate any of the window exercises into doors and apply as needed to fit the situation.

Serial jobs

Create a timeline, a long skinny narrative piece or a series of works about all your past jobs, individually and in order.

Combine all of your past job experiences into one big messy or desolate scene.

Identity

Look at the ideas concerning tags in the last chapter and apply them as they relate to having just left or lost a job. Think about the concept of relating job title to identity, and how we are so easily labeled.

Create a series of tags for all the jobs you have had. You can label them with your actual job title or with a more metaphorical version of how the job felt to you. Make a very tagged article of clothing you can wear, or a multi-tagged hat, or portray yourself as covered in these tags.

Using the same metaphorical interpretation of your job, create a plaque for your desk, a title for your door and embroidery for your shirt pocket.

Sometimes when you lose a job, you also lose your identity. Where did it go? Did you accidently leave it behind? Are you somewhat relieved that it is lost? Portray the search for your missing identity. Portray yourself as shedding the skin of your old identity with another fresh new identity replacing it from underneath.

Cleaning out your desk

Like filling a cardboard box with your job stuff the day you leave, fill an actual box with real or symbolic things representing leaving or losing a job. You can turn this box sideways and make a diorama. You can also decorate the outside of the box to enhance or contradict any meaning.

Imagine a box filled with your dignity, and carrying it out of there. What kind of box would that be, and what exactly would be contained inside?

Falling in Love

Falling in love elements and concepts – Crush, attraction, chemistry, walking on clouds, nervousness, butterflies, exhilaration, goosebumps, falling, melting, opposites, complimentaries, joy, focus and the rest of the world disappearing; hearts and flowers, boxes of chocolate, gifts, love notes

Valentines

Create unusual valentines for all kinds of occasions. Below are a few ideas:

- Use any color for your valentine besides pink and red
- Make a valentine out of seemingly harsh materials such as sheet metal or pieces of broken glass
- Create hybrid valentines using typical colors and symbols from other holidays, such as Halloween orange and black
- Design a matching set of valentines, each one expressing a different emotion

Love letters

Do the same as valentines above for love letters.

Set a trail of actual love letters for someone, like a scavenger hunt with clues. This could be a participatory performance-based installation piece.

Make a construction with hidden compartments, or a collage with flaps and pockets, all filled with love notes.

Make a piece of artwork in any style, in any medium, as though it were a love letter. As a challenge, don't use any actual alphabetical letters.

Crushed

Why is a crush called a crush? Is it because you often feel crushed while having one? Do a portrait of yourself in the throes of an intense crush. Are you being crushed by something bigger than you?

Do a piece of artwork in any style, medium and dimension about other crushed stuff, like crushed ice. For example, crush a stale loaf of bread with a brick, and then do a painting of it.

Up in the clouds

Paint or draw clouds exactly as you see them.

Create imaginary and metaphoric love clouds in two or three dimensions, in any medium.

Do a piece of artwork about walking on clouds, or floating among them.

Butterflies

Symbolically fill your stomach with butterflies. Don't actually eat them! Do a self-portrait about being deep in the state of love-shy nervousness, with a belly full of butterflies.

Portray yourself as covered with all kinds of butterflies, real and/or imaginary.

Depict and/or create special love-butterflies. Think about the qualities that set them apart from other butterflies. Did they start out as caterpillars? Do they go through the chrysalis process?

Make a wearable butterfly outfit for yourself or someone else.

Falling

Depict yourself or someone else as literally falling in love. At what rate of speed is the fall? In what sort of place or thing do you land?

Do an abstraction on the sensation of falling. As a challenge, include mostly horizontal lines and spaces in your composition.

Science

Express the chemistry of infatuation as though it were a science experiment. Fill vials, bottles and jars with love potions, colored water, rose petals, laundry lint (sometimes that's what is appropriate for the situation), and other such things.

Use actual magnets in a piece of artwork to express attraction and repulsion.

Portray any of the above ideas in a two-dimensional piece including at least two figures.

Melting

Portray yourself as melting and dripping.
Portray yourself as a puddle.
Portray other melting things.

The embrace

Portray inanimate things wrapped around each other in an embrace. You can work in any medium, with any materials, and in any style. Below are three ideas to get you started:

- The delicate tendrils of a bean plant wrapped around a nearby sunflower stalk

- A telephone cord wrapped around a boot, whose laces are wrapped around the body of the phone

- Create three-dimensional abstract shapes that are wrapped around each other. For example, using two colors of clay, make two non-specific forms and have them embrace.

Flowers

Of course, you can always do the classic, representational painting of a bouquet of flowers or a single elegant rose.

Or you can depict an abstraction of flowers. Have a maximum of three colors of flowers, no more than a 20% level of realism, and have at least three flowers go off the edge of the picture plane.

Create flowers out of any material, the more unusual and strange, the better. For example, make flowers out of buttons, safety pins and elastic. You can also try making flowers from old electronic parts, pipe cleaners and wax paper.

Make bouquets out of things besides flowers. I have often referred to a bunch of old paint brushes banded together as a bouquet.

Chocolates

Make dividers inside a box and fill it with other things, edible or not, that are either expressive of love or a broken heart.

Think about the shape of a box of chocolate, which is usually rectangular or heart-shaped. What else could the box be?

Chocolate – now there's a medium! Take a chocolate-making workshop. Create edible art. Yum!

Goosebumps

Portray the sensation of goosebumps. Depict the prickly texture and feeling of goosebumps in an abstract manner.

Do a self-portrait as a goose.

Learning to Ride a Bike

Bike riding elements and concepts – Tricycle, training wheels, helmet, balance, physics, wheels, spokes, spinning, tires, metal, rubber, shiny; bike style, color, embellishment; sense of flying, speed, freedom; falling over, wobbly, unsteady, pedaling, coasting, braking; riding in circles, going around the block, riding through puddles

Pedaling and cycling

Do an abstraction based on the motion of pedaling, cycling and spinning. As an extra challenge, don't use any circular shapes.

Think of the meaning of the word cycle; circular, going through cycles, the cycle of life. Do a free-writing session on the idea of cycles and circles. What sort of word-images come to you, and what can you create from them?

Two wheels, or not

Think about the design of the tricycle; three wheels based on the triangle. Design and/or create a tricycle that is based on even more triangles, to make a very triangular type of tricycle. Say that last sentence five times fast.

Design a uni-bi-tri-etc-cycle. Have one really big wheel, a medium wheel and a really small one, or maybe five tiny little wheels. Attach wheels in odd places. Create an octocycle.

Bicycle design

Design bicycles with new functions. Have one that automatically goes in circles, or only in reverse. How about a bicycle that keeps you dry while riding during rainy days?

Come up with new ideas for training wheels, both aesthetic and functional. Think about the concept of the training wheel.

Aesthetically design a bicycle based on anything besides the bicycle. Here are some ideas you can use:

- Other modes of transportation such as boats, cement mixer trucks, or rocket ships
- Birds; buzzards, hummingbirds, roadrunners, pelicans and robins
- Any other living creature, from mammals to reptiles to fish
- Kitchen items such as teacups, spoons, cheese graters or colanders

The manual

Create a how-to-ride-a-bike manual as an artist book. Use collage, assemblage or make the manual as an illustrated cube in any material you choose.

Old bicycle parts

Make a non-functional, abstract assemblage sculpture almost completely out of old bicycle parts.

Make a new kind of wheeled vehicle-type-thing from at least 75% old bicycle parts that has the ability to go somewhere.

The view going by

Depict pieces of the actual view that you see while riding your bike. Create a series of individual pieces or combine them all into one continuous narrative.

Portray the view as it is seen whizzing by, as opposed to the static views depicted in the above exercise. Try to make this as realistic as possible.

Create one or more fictional bicycle-riding views for your own entertainment. What would you really like to see as you ride your bike through the neighborhood? Is there a metaphorical view of what is actually there? How about the view of a strange abstract world with bike trails (unless, of course, your city still sees bike trails as a strange and abstract concept).

Puddles

Riding through the puddle paddle poodle with a saddle, wait a while make you smile through the turnstile. Hey won't you come away through the day, rainy painy very wet make a mess, splash and spray throughout the day. Make a trail on the setting sail, see the scales of the bike track tail.

Imagine riding your bike through puddles, the splash and spray and the trail of water leading out. Write something evaporative, and therefore, very temporary.

Make a puddle of ink on paper. Move the ink around with any kind of writing utensil or other tool.

Do a free-write similar to the above and see what word-images and ideas come to you.

Embellishments

Go to any bicycle shop, and you will see they are not just selling tires and helmets. Domestic bikes need embellishments (well, sort of). Okay, they are not really necessary (except for lights and reflectors), but they can be expressive. Redesign any of the following bike accessories purely for the fun of it. Add to your bike as aesthetically needed.

- Baskets and panniers
- The seat
- Lights and reflectors (safety first)
- Those fringe thingies that come out of the handlebars
- Water bottle
- Snack bar

Finding Inspiration
in Various States of Being

Introduction

Emotions are a natural process. They are an essential part of our humanity. Emotional states of being are a magnificent source of inspiration for artwork. Some of the most powerful art is imbued with strong emotion.

Although some emotions may be hard to endure, none are inherently bad, as long as they are neither misdirected nor suppressed.

Releasing emotion through the arts is an extraordinarily constructive thing to do. We let others know they are not alone, whether through sharing our joy or releasing our pain. Telling our stories through creating art, expressing tough emotions abstractly, or drawing them out exactly as they are, is often key to alleviating that which haunts us. Celebrating the wonders of experiencing life through the visual metaphors of art is equally important. This has the potential to become visual creativity at its finest. And the most painful emotion, expressed well, can inspire positive action.

The sections in this chapter, each based on a primary emotion, are in alphabetical order. I have written a little bit about each emotion or state of being, with a few suggestions that you can use for creating artwork. After that, you will find a set of specific guidelines for portraiture based on each emotion, in case you desire some structure.

The portraits can be of yourself, someone you know or someone that is completely imaginary. The abstractions are for any medium. The craftwork options are more geared to craft mediums and approaches, but anything can be applied to anything else. The challenge options are for giving yourself a tougher bone to chew, where you are still aiming to express that particular emotion or state of being, while utilizing typically contrary visual elements.

If I say to use two colors and black, then I mean that you can use black and any two colors, such as red and purple. One color, red for example, means that you can use all types of red; warm, cool, dark, light, brick, tomato, blood, scarlet or cherry red. Any red will do, and all reds equal one color (i.e. red) for these exercises. Therefore you will have black, along with a whole range of reds and a whole range of purples, or whichever two colors you choose.

Comfort

To have a sense of comfort is to be soothed from pain or fear. It is when you are made comfortable and put at ease in the presence of anxiety or in the aftermath of some sort of hurt.

The second syllable of the word comfort is fort. A fort offers a sense of security in the face of a real or perceived threat, and that sense of security can bring great comfort to someone who is fearful. Design a comfortable and comforting fort. Create an installation of a fort that is easing you from any fears, pain or anxiety that you or someone else may have. Use appropriate materials in your fortress installation. For example, in reaction to a child's ballet mishap, create a small fort where the bandaging gauze is tulle in soothing colors, the inside walls are a soft satin, and multiple ribbons hang sweetly. Make it a safe protective place where only happy ballet adventures reside.

Comfort food is bowl food (unless of course it is a chocolate bar, which could be broken up and placed in a bowl). Make bowls that are especially meant for soothing a disheartened soul. Give them love handles. Use classic bowl mediums such as glass, ceramic or carved wood, but also experiment with things like yarn or paper if those materials suit you better.

Make physically and emotionally comfortable soft sculpture. This would be like creating odd and interesting pillows especially meant for comforting someone. Give your sculptural pillow arms to wrap around a person. Maybe it has an attached quilt or blanket for warmth, or a cup holder for tea or cocoa.

Create something, abstract or not, from bandages, gauze and other symbolically healing materials. Make a really big bandage out of anything, but make it big enough to be of sufficient comfort to heal.

Do portraits of people (or other creatures) being comforted or giving comfort. This is different from the portrait guidelines below, which are for expressing a sense of comfort.

Comfort guidelines

Regular portrait – The person being portrayed is wrapped in something or being embraced by somebody.

Challenge portrait – The person being portrayed is all alone.

Regular abstract – Have two or more forms and lines being wrapped, held, or cupped like a bowl. Do not depict the idea of serenity. Instead, show some pain being soothed, and maybe beginning to heal. Include both rough spots and smooth areas.

Challenge abstract – Have no more than three curves of any kind. Make sure that the piece is at least 80% angular, sharp, and pointy. Use only two colors and black.

Craftwork – Use soft materials to make real quilts and shawls, or abstracted non-functional comforting things. If you work in hard materials, then make bowls or other things that envelop. Create something to give to someone, to help comfort them. Use any guidelines that you choose.

Confidence

Confidence is not to be confused with arrogance, but comes from a realistic assessment of your own personal power and abilities. When you are confident, you know for a fact that you are just fine with the issue at hand. You are secure enough in this knowledge that you do not need to put anyone else down in the process.

With a sense of confidence you are strong, sure and steady. You can walk into a room without any worries or self-consciousness. Like the mountain that sits in place, the running river and the blowing wind, you are doing what you were born to do without question or doubt.

As an artist, it would be wonderful to have complete confidence in your creative and technical abilities. In order to get there you need to have enough confidence in yourself to make mistakes, to not need to always be brilliant, and to not know or have to be good at absolutely everything. Being confident is not the same as being perfect. The goal of perfection can paralyze you with the fear of failure. Fear is the enemy of confidence.

I didn't learn that much about painting the first time I went to art school (which is another story altogether). However, I do remember one teacher from that school who made a great impression on me. This was a beginning painting class. He told us to give ourselves the freedom to make mistakes. He wanted us to make "big, bold, beautiful mistakes" so that we could learn from them. Hopefully, we would not repeat any of those mistakes, but instead find new glorious mistakes to make and, consequently, learn from. This is how we built confidence in our abilities, and at the same time, learned to love the act of painting. With experience at anything, you will become more confident. By taking chances with your art, whatever those aesthetic risks may be, your work will eventually grow stronger. If you believe that you can only do one thing well, and therefore you should continue to do that one thing only, then you display a lack of confidence in your own creativity. Push yourself beyond your own boundaries, and although you may create some strange and not-so-good art along the way, you will eventually discover that you have abilities you never thought possible. When you realize that you can achieve new things through your own power and determination, you will become confident, and so will your artwork. Enough said.

Confidence guidelines

Regular portrait – The person is shown upright, front and center, and looking straight at the viewer. Use at least two primary colors somewhere in the painting; on the figure or in the background.

Challenge portrait – Place the person being portrayed in the bottom third of the painting, or so far over to the side that at least one third of the figure is off the picture plane.

Regular abstract – Use only black, white and a maximum of four primary and/or secondary colors (red, blue, yellow, green, orange, purple). Have the main activity of the abstract be centered, both horizontally and vertically.

Challenge abstract – Have 80% of the main visual activity be way off to the bottom or over to one side. Have an element of something that is mostly hidden, or describe a general sense of things being hidden.

Craftwork – Choose one strong bold color, with or without slight variations on that color. Have that color be at least 75% of the piece. Combine three strong forms or shapes as the predominant feature of the piece.

Confusion

Being confused is when your mind is in a twist. Make that a double or triple twist. You are bewildered and perplexed. The inside of your poor head is in a state of serious disorder. Any sense of clarity has up and left.

The first syllable, con, often means against. The second two syllables, fusion, means that which is fused together, the parts becoming the whole. Therefore con-fusion, is against any sort of unity. When you are in a state of confusion, your particles of thought are scattered about. There they go.

To express confusion visually, you could portray a combination of too many things at once. Make something in at least a few different mediums, using as many materials as you can, and make it in as small a space as possible. If you already work in mixed-media, then apply as many layers as the support will hold. If you work two-dimensionally, then use an outrageous amount of colors at once. Go past colorful. Use so many colors that it almost looks gray from a distance, but not quite. Go for enough clutter that it is a mess, but not so much that it becomes a pattern.

You could aim for visual clarity, but express confusion in meaning. Depict a few things going on at once, but with too many possible interpretations. This is a good use for old unresolved pictorial work. Take what you have done so far, and add stuff that has little to do with the original picture. Do not obscure the original picture too much. Add another element that barely relates with what you have depicted so far. You are not aiming for absurdity, but confusion, to have some truly vague sense of meaning, but then again, not quite. It shouldn't really mean anything, but does hint slightly at having some meaning, just for confusion's sake.

An example of the above would be a simple formal portrait, with a lake at sunset brushed over parts of the portrait, and then have a pair of rodeo clowns walking through the landscape. Or maybe you have an unfinished war scene, so you paint in half a vase of flowers. Then you add the outline of a bright yellow cartoon duck. What could it all mean?

Hey kids! Want to confuse them at your next painting critique? Do the above and keep a straight face.

Being confused is like having an eggbeater whirring away inside your head. It's all a big tangled knot; spaghetti on the rampage. Express this mental mess by creating work that is scribbly and incongruent. Do you work in fiber? Make the biggest, most impossible knot that you possibly can. Create something out of knots of wood.

Make layers of things obscuring other things. Portray fogginess. Use semi-transparent veils in two or three-dimensions to confuse what may or may not be there.

Confusion guidelines

Regular portrait – The person is not looking straight ahead. Their outfit, hat or glasses are not on quite right. There is a cluttered room or landscape in the background.

Challenge portrait – The person is looking directly at the viewer, and there is a plain background. The background and person's clothing are limited to two colors.

Regular abstract – Make a mess of perspective, with plenty of random lines and masses, like Pollock meets Escher, but the disorganized version. Have no visual cohesion. (Hint: Pollock's work was cohesive, with an all-over pattern.) Use as many colors as possible.

Challenge abstract – Do an abstract that is geometric; mostly right angles and simple shapes, similar to Piet Mondrian's later work. Use a maximum of three colors, plus black and white if you like.

Craftwork – Mix at least five different materials and at least eight different colors (including black, white and gray). Have the piece clash visually with itself. Make it appear to have a function, but have that function not be the least bit functional.

Curiosity

Curiosity is defined by the persistent quest for knowledge. A curious person wants to know things, not out of nosiness or intrusiveness, but for the sake of understanding the world. Someone in an actively curious frame of mind will seek different ways of viewing and comprehending things, and will not simply accept the surface presentation of whatever it is.

Curiosity is a force for continued growth as an artist. What about this, what if I try that, what if I look at this some other way? What if that shade of green is slightly different, or if this tree bends the other way, or if it is dusk instead of the middle of the day, or if I use six lines here instead of five over there? Imagine if I made weavings out of clay instead of fiber, or if I added colored wire to my drawings, somehow. Curiosity keeps pushing the imagination and gives life to constant variation.

Make art that is about asking questions. Don't give away any answers, but leave any possible meaning open-ended, so that viewers may come to their own conclusions. Create curious work. Use interesting materials, show new ways of looking at things, take an unusual approach to your medium. You are not looking to create confusion. Do not make a mess. Just make something a little odd or open-ended, whether in meaning, material or aesthetics.

Curiosity guidelines

Regular portrait – Show something mysterious or unusual in the background. Have one eyebrow raised on the person's face.

Challenge portrait – Do a straightforward, no-expression portrait with a plain background.

Regular abstract – Create a composition that is neither overly simple nor complex. Have at least one element overlapping another, and include a twist (use your own definition of twist, whether visual or in meaning).

Challenge abstract – Do a color field piece. Have a minimum of 90% of the surface be one relatively solid color.

Craftwork – Use three contiguous colors (from the color wheel) such as green, yellow-green and yellow, and one other color that is complimentary to one of the three, such as red-violet. Have the piece appear to be one thing, while functioning as another, such as a vase that is really a pillow. Curious, yes?

Exhaustion and Fatigue

These are both states of extreme physical and/or mental weariness due to overexertion or illness. With exhaustion and fatigue you feel completely drained, like you have nothing left to give to yourself or anyone else.

Preparing for an exhibition with a tight deadline can leave you worn out and needing patches. There will be times when you will be too tired to go into the studio. Sometimes you just have to push yourself, so that you will get past the point of exhaustion and hopefully catch a second wind. Sometimes you just have to go and take a nap.

Portray someone or something as literally being drained and emptying out. Show something as drooping or melting, not from heat, but from lethargy. Fatigue is not blank, but emits a heavy feeling, an opaque heaviness in color and feel that is heading towards the bottom. Exhaustion is a sense of being depleted, with energy leaving or already gone.

Depict a landscape with everything almost horizontal, not dead, but lying down. Have a reclining figure so tired that they are sinking into and below the settee. Paint a flat navel orange, so overwhelmed with fatigue that it cannot possibly be round anymore.

Exhaustion and fatigue guidelines

Regular portrait – Place the person's face below center and/or off to side, but not off the picture plane. Use at least 50% different shades of gray, both warm and cool.

Challenge portrait – Use lots of bright, cheery colors for the person's clothes and in the background. Locate their face above center.

Regular abstract – Have most of the weight of activity sit below center. Use at least a 75% minimum of grays and browns in your piece.

Challenge abstract – Make a composition be at least 90% of the following colors; yellow, orange, red, pink, white and warm light brown. Include lots of circular shapes and forms.

Craftwork – Create something that is bottom heavy and is desperately fighting to be vertical, but has little choice to be anything but horizontal. Use mostly dull, tired and opaque colors.

Frustration

Frustration comes when something you are trying to do refuses to be done. You are spinning your wheels. You put all your effort into going somewhere, but instead you get nowhere. When you put a lot of work and effort into something, and you both desire and expect results, you become frustrated when nothing happens.

Creative blocks, of course, can be a major source of frustration to an artist. Hopefully, this book is helping to alleviate that. Uncooperative tools and materials, career roadblocks, exhibition rejections, lack of sales, as well as most anything else in life, can be extremely frustrating.

Thinking of the word frustration brings to mind pushing, tension and resistance. Which then brings to mind rubber bands, springs, solid pieces of apathetic rock, and small sheets of wire screen. Don't ask. Dunno. But whatever you see when you think of being frustrated, make something of it, either as subject matter or material.

You can physically express frustration in the process of making art, depending on the medium you use. Venting frustration on a large canvas is a healthy thing, as is slamming the air out of a lump of fresh clay. Expressing frustration in glass is probably not a good idea, unless you can think of some way to safely do so. The last thing you want is to hurt yourself, and therefore become even more frustrated.

A more difficult approach is to carefully create something that shows the feeling of frustration, while not physically venting it in the process. Instead, this would be a mental release of frustration. For example, you can depict a frustrating incident, carefully tie lots of knots where they don't belong in a weaving, or you can try any of the portrait ideas below.

Compositions that are not quite resolved can be frustrating. Take that piece of work in progress that has been driving you crazy and instead of resolving the poor thing, purposefully make it even worse. Make it as awful and uninspiring as possible.

Frustration guidelines

Regular portrait – Portray the person with their face in a twist, or with their cheeks bloated. Use a few diagonal visual elements that are pushing against something else. Include a sense of resistance to the piece.

Challenge portrait – Have the person be smiling. Place flowers in the foreground. And in the background create a serene beach or lake scene, with or without a sunset.

Regular abstract – Place two sets of visual elements that are both resisting each other and are hopelessly knotted together. Use colors that are close in tone, but that clash with one another.

Challenge abstract – Base your composition on a minimum of five horizontal, wavy lines in sweet pastel colors.

Craftwork – Make something that is fighting with itself, or that seems unfinished even though it is actually a completed piece. For example, a beaded necklace with some purposeful, but not symmetrical, knots and a few significant beads missing from the pattern.

Fury

Fury evokes a certain fierceness, an unrestrained rage, often born out of a passionate conviction. And for some reason, I think of wild horses, but I cannot recall the connection. Therefore, I did a short free-writing session on the subject of fury:

Fury running all over in lines and circles without symmetry, running wild rampant amok. Steam venting through every pore screaming until you're sore. Crazy rage. Don't turn the page. Fury comes from unjust circumstances, unfair chances, mama tiger poked and prodded. Anger stands still, throws darts, gives the evil eye. Fury is the storm around that eye. Fury rages like hurricanes gone off course. Herds of outraged horses hoofing up the dust storms.

To do a work in realism, approach the idea of furiousness with an abstract frame of mind. Design a composition with a sense of uncontrollable, spinning outrage. Even as a pure abstract, this is not easy, but is an effort well worth trying, especially if you are actually feeling furious about something.

Even when things are going well, and you are mostly a happy person, dealing with things like automated phone systems can raise fury. Yelling at the machine on the other end of the call usually does not help. But you can collect old telephones and pieces of wire and create something that expresses just how you feel about the whole system.

I began to compose a painting a number of years back that was going to be called The Sound of Our Discontent. At the time I lived near an airport, and for the better part of a year, while the main runways were closed for repair, they routed all the planes and jets over our neighborhood, and directly over the apartment I was renting. Stepping outside, looking straight up and screaming at airplane bellies didn't do much good. So I began planning this painting. But within a few months I moved a mile or so away, the main runways reopened, and I soon had more pressing things to paint.

Fury guidelines

Regular portrait – The person's face is partially blurred and twisted. Use high contrast, predominantly hot colors such as orange and red, and lots of lines and brushwork.

Challenge portrait – Utilize low contrast and cool colors with a soft background. The person's eyes and mouth are closed.

Regular abstract – Create a large piece that includes multiple lines, masses, open curves, angles, diagonals, high contrast and hot colors. Don't have it be so cluttered that you create a pattern. Leave some breathing space in the composition, but not too much.

Challenge abstract – Make a small piece with low contrast, cool colors, few horizontal or vertical lines, and include between one and three flat massed areas.

Craftwork – Make something with broken parts. Make a collage out of torn paper, with pictures and headlines that infuriate you. Be messy with the glue. Make a necklace out of broken beads, buttons and shells. Leave lots of loose threads. Make a "functional" ceramic piece, like a vase or a bowl that is very lopsided, has rips and tears in the clay, and is glazed mostly, but not completely, in red and black. Here is a bowl that is furious.

Happiness

This is all that most of us want. Yet at times, being happy can seem so elusive. Happiness is often characterized by serenity and contentment. Being happy connotes joy and delight in response to something.

Some of the strongest art, in my own opinionated opinion, comes from conflict and tension. My creative writing teacher once told us that much of literature is concerned with the basic issues of life and death, including fairy tales where animals must find food or they will die. I suppose, it is the resolution of problems, along with the knowledge and understanding of the difficulties of life, that clarify what happiness is by contrast.

I have often said that when I am happy, I am too busy savoring the feeling to create art about it. But I have nothing against others creating happy art. Not to be confused with beauty, which can co-exist with any emotion, happiness expressed in art can bring joy to the viewer. And many of us do hope for and greatly appreciate a happy ending to a story.

The challenge is to make happy art without it being trite. If the emotion is genuine for you, then express exhilaration, giddiness, light and free laughter, giggles and smiles to your heart's delight.

You could also push expressions of happiness to an extreme; overly cheerful and downright goofy, like a soft explosion of confetti, the details of a child's birthday party with the clowns and balloons and daisies and colorfully frosted cake. Fill your work with happy colors, all light and bright and no shadows.

Happiness guidelines

Regular portrait – The person is smiling, their eyes are sparkling, and the background is sunny during the day and well-lit at night.

Challenge portrait – There is a dark background, especially during the day. The person's face is half in shadow and they are not smiling.

Regular abstract – Have the basis of the composition be dots, circles, bubbles and vertical lines. Use an 80% minimum of light and bright colors.

Challenge abstract – Use at least 75% dark colors, and have two large squares as the predominant compositional feature.

Craftwork – Use colors, forms and materials that make you happy, and that resonate well with you. Do not create this piece to please anybody else under any circumstances. Make something gorgeous and fun that you get to keep for yourself, for your own collection or personal use.

Sadness

And then there is sadness, a somber unhappiness. It is such an unfortunately universal emotion, that artwork expressing a state of sadness will touch many people. Created from genuine experiences and/or observations of sorrow and grief, such art has the ability to transcend language and culture.

A simple free-write:

Sadness drips in many-sized drops, tick tock time is an immediate thing, minor key slow sing. It is still and pained and dark and stained. Deep and slightly transparent, it is easy to wear it. Single distant bell chimes, away so far away. Melancholy bare trees, with minimal signs of life, dragged under by strife.

The state of sadness comes in cool colors and grays with a transparent heaviness. It is an overcast day, a slow drizzle, a bleak and distant landscape, even if that bleak view is looking the long way down a deserted city street. It is lonely as a solitary mourning dove on a telephone wire. Sadness is a tear that begins at the surface and becomes a chasm deep inside. It is a rock, worn smooth over time by wind and water, but always there, becoming a subtle, yet constant, pebble in your shoe.

If you have an old sadness gnawing at the fragments of your days, then write about it. If your grief is recent, expressing it in words can help to relieve some of the pain. As artists we are very fortunate. We have this extraordinary means of expressing our sadness.

Write about sadness, if you need to clarify and create word-images. Or go straight to the canvas (or any other material) and express your grief, your crushed and hollow feelings, in any manner as you see fit.

Sadness guidelines

Regular portrait – The person has downcast eyes, they are placed low or off to the side, and they are wrapped in something. The background is bleak and the contrast level is low.

Challenge portrait – Use mostly mid-range primary and secondary colors. The person's gaze is in the direction of the sky or the ceiling. Include some colorful foliage in either the background or foreground.

Regular abstract – The composition has a focus on the bottom half. Use 95% cool and neutral colors, at least 40% transparency and a general sense of low contrast.

Challenge abstract – Use bright colors in high contrast. Include a significant amount of swirls and simple geometric shapes.

Craftwork – Focus on cool, transparent colors, low contrast, and simple solitary things. Give the piece a bottom heavy, drooping, downward motion, and a sense of distance. For example, a sad quilt might be mostly in shades of gray-blues, with a few pale, cool, green patches and dark gray stitching. The pattern of the quilt would be off-center, and not the least bit symmetrical. It might have a heavy filling (by weight), be thin in some areas and be purposefully frayed along an edge or two. Sad, sad quilt.

Finding Inspiration in Dreams

A Little Bit About Dreams

Dreams are an extraordinary source of artistic inspiration. They are pure creativity unto themselves, presenting new worlds to us on a nightly basis. Through dreams we can be someone else, meet new creatures, visit exotic places, have powerful abilities, and see everyday life through new sets of eyes. I am an intense dreamer, and my dreams have a profound effect on my art. Your dreams can do the same for you.

There are many differing views and a grand assortment of theories on the nature of dreams and the purpose, if any, that they serve. Personally, I believe that there are many diverse types of dreams that we may have for any variety of reasons.

Clean-out-your-head Dreams

These are the kind of dreams where you review your day. Clean-out-your-head dreams are composed of events that may have occurred recently, things that you have been thinking about, either consciously or subconsciously, that surface in the dreaming mind. Some things in your dream may be disguised as other things. Who knows why.

Do a busy, cluttered piece inspired by a clean-out-your-head dream. Include a few pictorial things that come to clarity through thin areas, cracks, seams and/or hidden flaps in the surface.

Make an assemblage or installation piece that is a cluttered mess of objects, and parts of objects, based on an actual dream that you have had. Try to find items from your dream at yard sales, flea markets and thrift stores. You can also collage or sew two-dimensional things representing elements from your dream.

Paint or draw a clean-out-your-head dream. Take something that should have made sense, like a vase of roses sitting on a table, but add all kinds of mysterious pictorial elements to create a fictitious dream. For example, replace a few of the rosebuds with tiny vacuum cleaners. Place monkey and clown portraits on the wall behind the vase. Peel back parts of the vase, with the water still in place where it belongs. Use three separate and distinct light sources. Have a few of the rose leaves turning into green caterpillars trying to crawl away through the air. Turn half of the thorns into little forks. Place a fire truck driving backward across the lace under the vase. Bonus – When the piece is done, you get to hear all kinds of fun and strange interpretations of your "dream".

Portray a series of individual elements from the same dream in any medium, in any format. For example, if the above was a real dream, then you could do individual small paintings of the clown, fire truck, tiny vacuum cleaner, green caterpillar, and so on. You could also make quilt-square pictures of the same things, or make separate ceramic pieces out of them to be used as a table setting.

Inspirational Dreams

Inspirational dreams come from our own deeper subconscious or our higher selves, or maybe even come from elsewhere outside ourselves in the spiritual realm. Some inspirational dreams that come to artists are specifically about artwork. If you are lucky, dreams can resolve technical and creative problems. A dream may show you the way to start or finish a difficult piece of artwork with which you have been struggling. You may see yourself creating work that you never would have thought of in your waking hours. In a dream, you may go to a museum where you see art that no one on earth has yet created, and this new art form may be a wonderful new path for you to take.

I have had this type of dream on occasion. One dream stands out for me, although it is now many years later. I was walking through a large hall, possibly a gallery or museum. A painting I had started was on the wall. It was still mostly raw canvas, but one corner was painted in deep layers of greens and metallics. I was able to see through each layer, so that I would know how to later reproduce this particular effect. And although it was a very simple scene, it has since affected some of the things that I do in the studio.

Precognitive Dreams

These are the sort of dreams where you dream about an event in advance of it actually happening during waking hours. Precognitive dreams are rare. I've only had one dream, that I remember, that could possibly be considered precognitive, and there was no way to know until after the fact.

If you think that you have precognitive dreams, record the dream and then write down the corresponding event as it actually happened later on. You can create split-comparison pieces based on your studies. You could also do a triptych; in the center place elements that the dream and reality have in common, on the left put the parts of the dream that did not play out, and on the right place the parts of the real event that were not represented in the dream.

Repetitive Dreams

Recurring dreams can easily inspire art. These are among the most interesting dreams for me. Working with repetitive imagery can help you realize the meaning of your dreams. No one else can really do that for you, unless they know you intimately, and even then, anyone else's interpretations are worth questioning. These dreams are yours.

When I was younger, I had a series of dreams about teeth crumbling. This is indeed quite a common theme, and can be very disturbing to the dreamer. These crumbled teeth showed up in a few paintings; one called Teeth and another called Archaeology (http://alexalev.com/book-references.html). In both paintings I used long rows of broken teeth as a visual element, adding meaning to the particular composition and story.

A more significant series of repetitive dreams lasted about five years, beginning early in 1996. I had a photograph of a chicken I had taken the previous September at the New Mexico State Fair. It was a grand chicken, and I wanted to do something with it. Then I had my first tornado dream; five tornados whirling across the open landscape in the distance. The tornados resolved my composition and gave it meaning. The chicken was placed in the foreground, its leg chained to a stake set in the ground. The tornados were placed menacingly in the background. The chicken could go nowhere, and could do nothing about the situation. The painting is called HEY CHICKEN! (http://alexalev.com/book-references.html) and is about not being taken seriously during times of crisis.

I have never seen a tornado in waking life, only benign and relatively small dust devils. In these recurring dreams, the tornados always came in sets of two or more. They were frequent for a few years, to the point where I was almost expecting to see tornados in my dreams, like, well, there they are. The tornados were off in the distance for the first few years, then they came closer, and by year four a few of these tornados passed directly overhead. Then they were off in the distance again, becoming less and less frequent. During this time I also had other water disaster dreams; floods, waterspouts, tsunamis, everything but a whirlpool. I took them all as a sign of deep emotional cleansing, you know, when a little soap and water just won't do. The water disasters all showed up in a number of paintings that I did from 1996 to 1998, and then I was done. I have other repetitive dreams as well, but they are mine and I love having them, as they are all enjoyable and interesting to me.

As said, repetitive dreams can be a wellspring of creative inspiration for any artist. Take your reoccurring dream or dream element, and apply any appropriate exercise in this book. For example, if you often dream of running dogs, then you could apply many of the exercises in Adopting a New Pet in the chapter titled; Finding Inspiration in Life Events. You may also find useful exercises concerning running dogs in other chapters, such as nature, visual elements or states of being. You can use running dogs instead of bees, doing laundry, or with seeing sound, if the running dogs in your dreams make a sound. Transpose one thing for another.

Here are a few things you can do with repetitive dreams:

You could create a whole body of work, especially for an exhibition, depicting these dreams whole and complete, or with simply using repetitive dream elements in other compositions (as I did with the tornados).

Create a series of small to medium-sized pieces, portraying the common themes and variations from one dream to another.

If you are primarily an abstract artist, then find the raw visual elements that the dreams have in common and work with that. For example, if you repeatedly dream of flying fish, then use the colors, the glossiness, the sense of speed and flight in your work. You can also create artwork using the words that represent the repetitive features of your dreams. For example, use the words; flying fish. See the chapter on language for more on this idea.

Paint one spectacular mural-sized painting (a minimum of five feet in any direction), or create a large three-dimensional piece in any medium, where you can work out the issues involved with your reoccurring dream in your waking hours. You can use images from these dreams, and also include your own interpretations of what they might possibly mean.

Nightmares

I am fortunate to have very few nightmares. I know that they can haunt people to the point of making them afraid to go to sleep. As an artist you are fortunate in that you can work your way through them by creating artwork about them. Face your fears. That is all that nightmares are. Through art you can have some control over nightmares, take back your power and consciously change the outcome of the dream.

Portray dream monsters as a way of confronting them. If there is one that haunts you, then portray it as extra scary, to the point of absurdity. Then do another portrait of the monster being sedate, cute and fluffy.

Depict yourself as hurrying through scary situations and places. Then give yourself a safe exit on the other side of the piece.

Do an abstract piece in the darkest, scariest colors, with lots of creepy lines and forms. Then ask yourself, why are these visual elements so scary? Darkness can be soothing to the soul and calming to the eyes. Think of sweet, summer nights when the moon is new, or in winter snuggled under layers of warm blankets pulled up over your head. Darkness can be comforting. Change your perception of seemingly scary elements into something benign and even lovely. Do both a scary piece and a soothing piece of abstracted artwork, each using at least 75% of the same visual elements as the other.

Incorporating-reality Dreams

In these types of dreams the story line is reflective of what is actually going on at the moment in the dreamer's body and physical surroundings. This may affect something you hear, feel or sense. For example, if you feel cold because your bedroom window was left open, you may dream of visiting Antarctica or being inside of a walk-in freezer. Maybe there are crows laughing wildly in your dream, when in reality your sister is down the hall watching a funny late-night movie on TV.

Maybe you have experienced dreams that incorporate reality into them. You can portray any of the sensations you experienced as pure abstractions, using color and other visual elements to express yourself, whether it is feeling hot, cold, hungry, crowded or itchy. This sort of dream also lends itself to split-comparison artwork, where you depict the scene in the dream alongside what was actually happening at the time, such as laughing crows and a giggling sister.

Telepathic Dreams

Not to be confused with precognitive dreams, telepathic dreams can be out-of-body experiences initiated while sleeping. They can also be ways of communicating with others, either alive or deceased. The idea of telepathic dreams is controversial for those who believe that all dreams are the inner workings of the mind, or maybe they are wishful thinking and nothing else. The idea of there being existence on another plane is disturbing to some, and that's okay. It's just not the case for everybody. However, I have experienced quite a few telepathic dreams myself in varying forms. They have a distinct feel to them from regular dreams, and therefore I know the difference.

If you have the sort of flying dreams that are, or seem to be, out-of-body experiences, then portray the landscape as seen from your new vantage point. How do telepathic dreams feel in comparison to other dreams? How do you know they are real?

Dream Interpretations

In my opinion, dream interpretations are neither Freudian nor Jungian, but are made of a different code for everybody. Most dreams are subconscious, and they use symbolic visual, as well as verbal, language. The meanings and interpretations of these symbols are varied. Nothing is necessarily consistent from person to person.

It might be interesting to look through any number of books and other resources to see the numerous, and sometimes contradictory, interpretations for the same dream symbol. You could do a piece incorporating multiple panels in response to what you find.

According to four different sources, the dream symbol of cat means unclean spirit, stomach trouble, mysteriousness, guilt, femininity and self-reliance. You could do a portrait of an imaginary cat that has all of those qualities at once. As another example, the dream symbol river means journey, circulatory system, sin, judgment, obstacles and dividing line. Imagine doing a long, thin piece about a river that changes course at certain intervals of distance, according to each of these different qualities.

You have your own dream iconography, and you will need to know it well in order to interpret your own dreams. Keep records of your dream elements; people, animals, places, objects, events, actions, etc., if you are not already recording the whole dream. If you know yourself well and feel like you can trust your own mind, then you can believe in your own interpretations. These things are not always static; they can change for you. People sometimes stand in for other people and scary things may seem oddly reassuring. I don't know why. That's just how it is.

When you are familiar with your own set of dream symbols, then you can work with them, including new ones that may seem curious to you at first.

Do a series of drawings, or other works, each with a different interpretation of the same whole dream or single dream element.

Do one piece of artwork that is a mix of your own possible and differing interpretations of the dream.

Create an installation, where the interior looks and feels like dream-space. Have the installation feature at least two different interpretations of the same dream. For example, if the dream took place in a forest, re-create that forest as best as you remember it. If the row of shore birds wearing party hats while waddling through the forest have two possible meanings for you, then include both of those meanings in your piece.

If you dream of something curious that you have never dreamed before, and it stays with you during the day, then the dream might have a message for you. Create a mysterious and questioning piece of art including that dream element or scene, and present all or some of the things you think that it might mean.

Lucid Dreaming

Lucid dreaming is when you are dreaming during sleep, but you are aware that you are dreaming while still inside the dream. Sometimes you can control events while you are in this state, and sometimes you can't, although you can exercise a keen observation just by being aware that you are dreaming. I have heard that one can learn to dream lucidly with practice. Often it just happens spontaneously. I have had a few infrequent experiences with this myself. Once during a rare nightmare of being chased, I suddenly realized that if I jumped up and down three times, I would wake up and get out of the situation. And I did.

Think of the control that we have as artists over the things we create. Although our materials and processes often have a mind of their own, depending on the medium, we still exercise quite a bit of control over a piece of creation. We think art into being, really. Every piece you create begins with something as intangible as a thought. When this thought is carefully and intently impressed upon physical matter, we have art, or whole buildings or yummy sandwiches or neatly folded stacks of clean towels. Imagine what we could do if we had control over our dreams; where we could fly to, what we could create, how we could perform.

If you can, and are lucky enough to be adept at lucid dreaming, try to create work beyond your current abilities in your dreams. Push what you already know how to do to greater heights. Try new materials and approaches to art-making. Successfully resolve that piece that has been driving you nuts for the past six months. Become the artist you strive to be. And when they say to you "in your dreams", you can tell them "no problem". If you can experiment this way with lucid dreaming, then do so. See how it affects your work in the studio during your waking hours.

Making Requests

This is when you ask to dream about something specific before falling asleep. Making requests is similar to lucid dreaming, but the control factor is made during the process of falling asleep, or just before, when you are relaxed in bed. You make the request while you are still conscious and aware of what you are asking.

You don't have to ask anyone in particular, but if you like, make the request of a higher power, your spiritual self, or a personal angel. You may dream about the subject that very night, or receive your answer a few mornings later. You may need to make repeated requests. You will probably remember the dream, but you might not, in which case the information will possibly filter through to your subconscious. It's worth trying.

Making requests of dreams can be useful in resolving artistic problems, especially since so much of what we remember about dreams is visual. We can seek guidance in creative, technical, and career issues through our dreams. Balance what you learn from these dreams with what you know to be true for yourself in waking life. You may not need to take any dream advice literally, but it may guide you to a better decision.

For example, let's say that you need to create an impressive sculptural piece for the entrance to a five-star restaurant. You request a dream that will give you some ideas for creative direction. Two nights later you dream about delicate metal scaffolding and pieces of shimmering broken glass in shades of green and violet that are knotted and hanging by silk strings. Upon waking, you realize this could be gorgeous and very striking, but difficult to create, as well as potentially dangerous for people to walk through and under. However, you could create something similar using stronger, unbreakable materials. You could give the illusion of delicacy, but make the piece safe to create, as well as safe for the restaurant clientele to experience. You may also decide to create something completely different, but still choose to work with the green, violet and metallic color scheme that was in your dream.

Dream Journals

Keeping a dream journal is an excellent way to collect all kinds of interesting word-images and ideas for imaginary scenes. Of course, keeping such a journal can also help you become more aware of your own repetitive dreams, dream elements and subconscious visual iconography.

You can use any old notebook, buy a journal specifically meant for recording dreams or you can make one. Be sure that you have one or two functioning pens at the ready. Do not lose your fading dream images by wasting valuable time and mental energy searching for a pen. Keep the journal and the pens by your bed, with a light and your eyeglasses if you need them. Record your dream immediately upon waking up. Alarms can be very disruptive to the recall process, they can wake you up too abruptly, but they are often necessary to get you up in time if you have to be somewhere in the morning. If you can, it is better to wake up naturally. Try this on your days off, when you don't have to worry about being late for anything.

Write down as many details of the dream or dreams as you can remember. Take note of any colors that you recall. Do not worry about grammar, spelling, interpretations or meanings. Do not be self-judgmental, and keep this notebook as private as any other journal. Don't forget to record the date. You might find it useful later on.

You can use the dreams in your journal similar to free-writing exercises for culling word-images. Here is a made-up dream as an example, followed by a list of word-images taken from the dream:

You are in a backyard garden, with small, black traffic lights sprouting as flowers in two rows by a brick wall. An orange-striped cat flies in, lands on one of the traffic light flowers and urgently licks one of its wings. Hearing a siren, you then notice a hospital building with smokestacks off in the near distance. Suddenly, you are sitting in a waiting room that is half-filled with stacks of old, ragged magazines. A pop hits cover band is standing on a low platform in the back of the waiting room. The four musicians, all middle-aged men, are playing a well-known song that you've never heard called; "Will You, Won't You, Window Fan". You go to get a drink from the water fountain, but the liquid is a thick, opaque, pale aqua-green color, and you are not sure what to do. It doesn't look safe to drink.

Sample imagery culled from this dream:

- Small, black traffic lights sprouting as flowers in two rows by a brick wall
- An orange-striped cat on a traffic light flower, urgently licking one of its wings
- A hospital building with smokestacks, off in the near distance
- Sitting in a waiting room that is half-filled with stacks of old ragged magazines

- Four musicians, all middle-aged men, standing on a low platform in the back of the waiting room

- The liquid from the water fountain is a thick, opaque, pale aqua-green color

Turning Dreams into Art

Surrealism, as an art movement, is notoriously linked with dreams. However, the true definition of surrealism involves the conscious realm as much as the subconscious. Waking life mixed and juxtaposed with fantasy, dreams, chance and odd views of the world combined together become a new reality that is visually expressed in surrealistic art.

Once, while in art school, I brought in a painting that was inspired by a dream for a class critique. The comments I received were "it doesn't look like a dream" and "make it more dream-like". I explained that my own dreams were extraordinarily vivid, and so very real to me at the time of having them. Nothing was dripping or melting, or resembled anything like the classic dream sequences in old movies. I wanted to depict my dreams as I saw them. That was much more of a challenge to me, and not the easy way out of being so stereotypical about it.

Be true to your own dream life. These are your visions; they belong to you and nobody else. If you wish to distort them in the service of your art, or change some parts, that is completely up to you. Following are some more ideas for creating artwork that is inspired by your dreams:

Portray a scene as real as you can remember it. Re-create all or part of the dream as if you were actually there. This is nowhere as easy as it sounds, and can be quite a challenge to reproduce the essence of your dream-space, no matter how real it felt at the time.

Portray the same dream scene as more confused, maybe layered with different viewpoints and images, including what you simplify from your dream looking back into it. You are not trying to re-create the exact feeling of being there anymore, but you are portraying the same imagery nonetheless.

The memories of most dreams are fleeting at best. Although a few rare dreams may stay with you all day, the rest hover around for a few minutes after waking and then they are gone, leaving only frail wisps of their former selves. Try to depict those fleeting wispy images before they are gone completely.

Reading about them in a dream journal can jog your memory enough to give you something to work with later on. Give your work the quality of something that is fleeting.

Use blurring techniques in your medium. Create something that has a sense of being blurred, or actually is blurred. Portray a real dream image that has been blurred or make a purely abstract or conceptual piece about the idea of blurriness.

Memories of dream scenes often blend together. Create a piece of artwork involving veiled transparent layers of different dream scenes.

Make diptychs and triptychs from dreams that you recall in two or more possible ways, as the details of your dream fade away.

Portray individual dream elements on their own, with no regard to the rest of the dream from which they originated.

Blend purely visual dream elements in with your other work. By ignoring any possible dream interpretations, you will be giving that element new life. Using an earlier example, you could take the dream element of the one flying orange cat, and instead portray five flying orange cats in a completely different setting.

Color in Dreams

As it turns out, most people do dream in color. Sometimes my own dreams have a sort of color-feel to them, without remembering any specific colors. For example, I had a dream early one morning with a sense of pastel blues, light greens and cool yellows dominating.

If keeping a dream journal is too much for you, then consider keeping a record a color notes from your dreams for a while. You can use these specific colors as the base for any of your non-dream creations. If you remember cinnabar orange, electric blue-violet and a rich, saturated red-purple as the color elements from your dream, you could easily apply those colors to stained glass, beads, yarn, fabric, ceramic glazes, as well as mixing the colors with paint, pastels and inks. This color scheme could be the dominant, or only, colors in any composition, with the subject matter having nothing to do with your dream. Yet by virtue of color, the resulting piece would still be dream-inspired.

Finding Inspiration
in Being Uninspired

The state of being uninspired can be a great source of inspiration if you let it. You just have to get into the moment, or the eternity-of-it-all, as it may seem at the time. You might just be feeling lazy for the day, or maybe you are going through a phase of unmitigated artistic hopelessness that lasts for months.

Put that hopelessness into your art. By virtue of giving expression to your despondency, you will be creating something. There you go.

Fear

Fear can hold you back from doing just about anything, and it can certainly knock the stuffing out of any creative impulse. Fear for artists can be reflective of technical inability, critical judgment, questions about meaning, and unfulfilled career expectations.

If you are afraid that your skill-level will never be very good, remember that even the most proficient artists in any medium had to start at the beginning. And that is not a pretty place, not for anybody. It takes a lot of hard work, years of practice, determination and plenty of serious play to master a new medium. At first, the results might not be all that much to look at. That's just how it is. No big deal. It's okay.

The only judge you need to be concerned with is yourself. Learn to honestly criticize your own work. Know that much of what you do as an artist is process and growth. Keep at it, and you'll be fine.

Listening to what others tell you to create can be stifling. If you feel like you want or need to grow as an artist, then please do so. It means taking risks, but these risks usually pay off. You may find a brilliant and engaging new direction in your art, or you may learn things along the way that help your previous work become even better than it was before.

It is one thing to have high standards for your finished work, and quite another to have such lofty intentions for every little thing you do.

Let it go. Let the fear go, and happily dabble in whatever captures your attention and piques your interest, no matter how seemingly mundane. Great meaning, beauty and innovation come with time, developed skill, and with lots of serious play. Brilliance comes when it wants to, but you cannot force it. Let go of the fear, get into the flow, and give inspiration the space it needs to make an appearance.

Time Out

Sometimes all you need to do is to take a little time off. Putter around in your studio, rearrange your art books, reorganize your materials, go to a museum, visit a friend, read a book, see a movie, or go take a walk in nature (fifty other people will also tell you to do this last thing, and they are right). Clear out your overstuffed head. Go see what life is all about. Not the annoying, scheduling, tiring car-tuning repairs, dentist appointments, bill paying, everyday get-in-line shuffle of life; but something more fun or soothing for your soul. Take a day off from obligations, both necessary and self-inflicted. Maybe, I will too.

Don't Obsess, Do Something

Don't think. Well, do some thinking. Enough to keep you out of trouble and keep that green paint out of the pink carpet. But not much more than that. This is when it is good to follow directions more or less to the letter. Use any of the exercises in this book and go play. Getting involved in a process without worrying about the results can open the doors to creative inspiration. You will be so busy using sponge stamps to create an abstract piece in blue, yellow and purple, on wood, involving the letter R, and with two puppy tails made out of clay, that all kinds of other ideas will find their way into your thoughts. And these ideas will lead you to something else altogether that just may resolve your lack-of-ideas for that mural project you agreed to do.

Get the Ball Rolling

Literally. Or not. Just start doing something creative. It doesn't have to be your regular thing, it just has to be creative. So create. Anything. Get the ball rolling.

Create spherical things. Knit small globes. Make detailed multi-colored clay marbles. Create a latticework sphere out of wire and twigs. Make balls out of hand-made paper.

Do paintings or drawings of spheres. Try to give these two-dimensional surfaces as much of the illusion of a sphere as possible. As a challenge, give these realistic-looking spheres surface patterns of any kind.

Design an intricate track system for metal, wood or glass marbles. If you are working with small metal balls, consider including magnets in the piece.

Qualities of Being Uninspired

Brainstorm on the word uninspired:

Bored, blank, nothingness, the void, emptiness, emptying out, space, holes, dullness, lackluster, beige, dust, stuck, walls, blocks.

And from these words come the rest of this chapter...

Bored

Boring, bore, board. Boar. A bored boar is boring holes in boards. You could spend all day just drilling holes, but that too could be boring. Ha ha, get it? Seriously though, you could make some interesting designs with holes in boards, make something out of found pieces of twigs and branches where insects have bored holes, or maybe create something out of pegboard. You could weave things in and out of the holes in a large piece of pegboard. This will keep you out of trouble.

Try to make the most boring piece of two or three-dimensional art that ever existed. Make sure that there is absolutely nothing interesting about it. This is more of a challenge than it seems.

Do a portrait, or a series of portraits, of people and other creatures yawning in boredom. Give them that glazed-over look.

The syllable -dom is a suffix referring to domain. So as there are king-doms, maybe there could also be a bore-dom, the domain of all that is boring. Depict a scene from the Land of Boredom, or if three-dimensionally inclined, create a royally boring installation.

Blank

The word blank is related to the Spanish and French words for white; blanco and blanche. I think of blank as being more of a clear with nothing on the other side, a continuous mirror world with nothing to see, over and over again, full of depth and nothing else. It can be defined by what it is not.

Work white on white. Make a collage, assemblage or mixed-media piece using only white materials and pigments on a white surface.

Work with colorless, transparent materials only. Include different levels of transparency, if you like.

Use stamps, sponges, opaque white ink, brushstrokes of white paint and so on to blank things out. This is the perfect use for any unfinished, bad pieces of art you have stashed behind everything else in your studio. Blank it out completely, or just cover parts of the surface in white. You may actually redeem the piece, or at least have some fun trying.

Do a self-portrait with a blank expression on your face. Either wear white and have a black background, or wear black and have a white background.

Nothingness

Which might be at most the remaining crumbs of toast, but less than that, an absolute zero. What does it take to leave nothing on the plate? Negative numbers, for example minus four, is that even more of nothing than there was before? If there is more of nothing than there is of plain old zero-type nothing, then can even more of nothing then at least be something? Is nothing only a flexible note as a relative term? If darkness is something, then what is the color of nothing? If it is clear, then what is over there?

After you have pondered these poetic questions, pay homage to nothingness and spend the rest of the day not creating anything, artwork or anything else.

For more of a challenge, try not to make any decisions either.

The Void

Devoid of anything, the dark hole, the abyss that goes on forever and ever and ever. Void. Empty. Deleted. In the pocket where you once placed a rock, a worn-out sock. Meaning nothing. A day in day out roundabout in and out. Nothing changes. A character-devoid void. A numbness. A stare. Nothing over there. Pulling a hollow out of a hat, imagine that. Shapeless, shiftless, nightshift, spring full of promise disappearing, the void, lack of knowledge, lack of knowing anything. One single sour note, hum, sing.

Do your own free-writing session on the subject of the void, or use any of the word-images culled from above:

- The dark hole, the abyss that goes on forever

- In the pocket where you once placed a rock, a worn-out sock

- One single sour note, hum, sing

Emptiness

Emptiness signifies a place or thing that once could hold, contain something, or something close to nothing, the void, the spaciousness of outer space, the disappointing cookie jar, a sweater long since worn, empty of a person's warmth, not just where nothing resides, but resounding of where something once was, but no longer is, a ghost town, an abandoned seashell, a dried-out well, nothing but a husk left out in the dust.

Do a free-write not to cull word-images, but to spark ideas for creating art. The exercises below were inspired by the free-write above.

Make a container that seems as though it has something in it, but upon closer inspection is really empty. Make something that should not be empty, but is.

Depict the vast emptiness in a scene, a landscape, or even a portrait.

Create an article of clothing that is impossible to wear, and therefore will remain forever empty of somebody to wear it.

Do a series of portraits of the ghostly inhabitants of a ghost town. This does not have to be the typical western ghost town, but it can.

Emptying Out

Portray a cheetah running at full speed, and then being depleted by exhaustion. Depict anything just barely running on fumes, stumbling, whimpering and slowly inching its way forward.

Do a self-portrait showing of all your creative brilliance pouring out of your shirt sleeves, your ears, your pant legs and generally leaving the premises. Portray how you really feel when inspiration takes a holiday.

Create a system that involves emptying something, sort of like plumbing, but in only one direction; out.

Space

The holy grail for artists, a part of the triumvirate: Time, money and space. Ah, the dream of more than sufficient studio space. A nice, large studio filled with all your art stuff, your complex flavor, your creativity. It is all a part of your realm, an extension of you, like an aura made of books, shelves, tables, supplies and most importantly, your creations, both finished and in-progress. Oh yeah...

Design your dream studio space, without any compromises, not even gravity if that is an issue for you.

Portray any of the following things having to do with space:

- Inner space; inside your physical or mental self

- Outer space; anything to do with astronomy

- Spaciousness; an abstraction depicting expansiveness, without it being a solid color field

- Spaciness; another abstract piece defining the qualities of being spacey, or somewhat out of it

- Space case; a portrait series of notable or imaginary spaced-out types of persons or creatures

Holes

Design or create a site-specific landscape piece involving holes and/or tunnels that are dug into the ground.

Create an assemblage piece made only with materials that have holes in them, such as; buttons, beads, pegboard, plastic donuts, metal rings, wooden hoops, or whatever else you can find in a craft supply store, hardware store or wherever else you might find hole-bearing items.

Make holes in a solid piece of hard or soft material; whether broken, ripped, torn, carved, drilled, scooped out or punched through.

Dots are the anti-hole. Create a collage or assemblage piece out of dot-like things such as stickers, shank buttons with the shank removed, glass medallions, round templates, circular pieces of wood, small metal disks and so on. Again, you will find all kinds of wonderful parts at craft supply stores, hardware stores, flea markets and yard sales.

Dull Lackluster Beige Dust

Very much like our old apartment, the rickety one where I wrote some of the earlier chapters in the original version of this book.

Try working with raw pigment, metallic powders and other dust-like materials. Don't forget to wear a face mask.

Do a two-dimensional piece about dust storms and dust devils. Dust devils are small tornado-like wind vortexes, usually found in hot, dry, sunny areas. We once saw a dog chasing a dust devil across a field in southeastern New Mexico. Now, that was entertaining!

What is the true color of being uninspired? Can it be found in beige-gray clutch purses, dull mauve pile carpeting, baby blue polyester dust ruffles, or pale orange plastic countertops? Create an abstract piece that is at least 90% in three of the dullest, most uninspiring colors in your opinion.

Portray a bleak terrain, a place where once was some sort of opulence, now gone dry for lack of use, such as a half-dead shopping center.

Collect old plastic beads, costume jewelry with missing rhinestones and broken clasps, silk scarves with stains, bent sequins, and create a wearable piece, or a whole outfit, that epitomizes long-faded glamour.

Take one or more shiny objects or materials and scratch most of the sheen out of it. Create something with these materials on the theme of the lackluster life.

Being Stuck

Stick incongruent things together, the more the better, to create an assemblage piece about being stuck. You can find water-based craft glue which is usually non-toxic, easy to use and holds very well, at most art and craft supply stores.

Portray things that are stuck, like a mouse in a trap or a zipper caught in a seam on the back of a cocktail dress.

Portray yourself as being metaphorically stuck. You feel stuck, so show yourself as being stuck in a doorway, in some fresh sidewalk cement, or in a trap of some kind.

Walls

Up against a wall, talking to a wall, hitting a wall. When you feel like your limits have been reached, the wall appears. Sometimes you will have to find your way around or over the wall, and other times you will need to dig your way under it. There will be times when you will need to painstakingly remove each brick one by one, until you can crawl your way through the wall. And then there will be those times when you need to take direction from the wall, and go somewhere else. Think of walls as a way of letting yourself know that you either need to be more determined or that you need to change direction. By no means stop, give up and/or park your defeated self at the base of the wall. That's not what they are there for.

Look at a wall of bricks. Notice all the shades of red. Which one of those colors is really brick red? Create an abstract piece using as many shades of brick red that you can imagine, from pale red-oranges to dark red-grays.

Create a bouquet of wallflowers, in any materials that you choose, and using any definition of wallflower that strikes your fancy.

Look into creating a mural. This could be a new direction for you, or simply a fun and enlightening one-time experience.

Paint an actual wall in an unusual way, with two or three separate colors, or maybe with a gradient or a surface texture.

Create a room divider, a temporary or moveable wall. Consider material, aesthetics, pattern, texture and any possible meaning.

Blocks

Create a physical block of time. Maybe you could use old clock parts, or play with numerical measurements of time in visual form. Make something you could place on a table and say "this is a block of time".

Do a painting of something as seen through glass blocks, in any style.

Concentrate on one city block. Take photographs of the things that you see on that one block and nowhere else.

Plan your ideal city block; a place where you could live, work, shop and play.

A blocked drain creates a clog, and prevents water from flowing. Build something out of pipes and other plumbing parts. Think about what could drain through them and what could be prevented from draining away. Is your creative flow clogged? Is it draining away? How can it flow, but not disappear forever? Will more inspiration come along to takes its place? Ponder these questions while making something from copper elbows, drain plugs and small rubber washers.

Remember those wooden building blocks from when you were a little kid? They either had the alphabet stamped onto their sides, or they were different brightly colored shapes. Blocks were fun. Make an assemblage piece out of old wooden blocks you find at the thrift store, or design a new set of wooden blocks for today's children.

Creative Blocks!

Make creative blocks. Literally. That'll teach them to mess with you. Take away their power over you by turning them into something else altogether. On the next page are a few ideas for making creative blocks:

Knit a brick. Use any soft fiber or material to knit, crochet, sew, knot or weave a cushy brick that looks like the real thing. Go for visual realism, with tactile abstraction.

Take a real brick and doll it up. Encrust it with fake jewels, buttons, beads, glitter and sequins. Maybe add some doll parts to the piece.

Start with a wooden block of any size or shape, and paint or draw related scenes or portraits on each side.

Wrap a cinderblock with different colored metallic foils. Then, wrap and weave different colored wire and ribbons through and around the holes. Add other materials if you like.

Carve intricate designs into small blocks of clay, akin to three-dimensional hand-made tiles.

Turn a watercolor block into an abstracted flip-book. Paint an abstract design in watercolor on the first page, and alter the design and color slightly as you continue to paint on each successive page. Then flip the pages and watch the show.

Watch a block of ice melt. Don't do anything else. Just observe the process. Notice color, clarity, transparency, shadow, highlight, the slowly spreading puddle and the changing form of the ice as it sinks lower and lower. Tell yourself how fortunate you are to be able to perceive such details the way you do, while truly appreciating the simple beauty unfolding before you.

The Musician Parallel

It's all about striking a balance. You do not have to do it all, nor do you need to narrowly focus all your creative output on just one thing. You neither have to be highly proficient at a dozen different methods and mediums to be considered creative, nor develop a brand to be an artist. I'm serious.

Your own style will come by your natural hand when you are comfortable with your materials. It can neither be forced nor falsely developed. If it is, the resulting artwork will be contrived. Be more concerned with knowing both your materials and technique well. Your own unique voice will come in time. What you have to say with that voice will also arrive when it is good and ready to be heard.

I have made the assumption that most of my readers work in a medium they know well and love. Maybe you don't. That's okay. If so, you have the freedom to try all kinds of things and not be concerned with taking time away from your more serious work. Maybe you can dedicate one whole year each for trying new mediums; this year clay, next year watercolor, and maybe cast glass the year after that. Or, if you are fortunate to have a good art center nearby, take random art classes that appeal to you. Eventually you will come across something; some method, material or process that sings beautiful songs to your soul.

Many artists (both historic and contemporary) have one primary medium. Yet, many of these artist also have another side thing that they do. There are sculptors that draw, painters that weave, photographers that knit, ceramicists that do calligraphy, and so on. The varieties are infinite.

Other artists who focus on one medium, just the same, continuously play with a variety of other methods and materials that strike their interest. Outside of their own specialty, the rest is simply artistic exploration. It's all part of the normal process of being an artist. Between curiosity and desiring a challenge, it is always fun to try new things. And everyone else's materials always look so intriguing and new and colorful!

Trying something new takes you outside of your usual self. If you are in a rut of any kind, then playing in another medium or taking a different approach with your usual methods can be healing. It is similar to being objective as opposed to subjective. There won't be so much at stake and it will be easier to get wonderfully lost in play. This is where magic can happen.

I am an oil painter first. There is no doubt about this. However, over the years I have explored many other forms of visual arts; watercolor, drawing, beadwork, fiber, paper arts, printmaking, ceramics, photography, mixed-media and installation. None of these other things have the hold on me that oil painting does. For me, they are avenues of play, where I can tap into other sorts of visual expression.

My second most consistent art form is writing lyric poetry; and studying music is still on my list. Some artists dance, some cook, some garden, and some do completely different things to round out who their creative selves are.

Years ago, we were listening to rare recordings of earlier popular songs; outtakes, odd versions of a few hits, exquisite snippets, near misses and pieces of musical mishaps. All were fascinating in their own context of being experimentation and pushing the limits of their times.

Listening to this music brought to mind the artist parallel. Whatever any of us creates, not all of it is going to be awesome. And some of it will only be amazing if we try all sorts of other things along the way. It's like brainstorming or free-writing, but using visual arts materials instead of words. Many strange things may be created, but that's cool. It's an important part of the process.

When the time comes that you can look back over years of creative work, you will see all kinds of fascinating things about your course of development. I once heard someone say; "You must paint 500 bad paintings before you can paint a good one." You have do your share of novice work to learn anything worthwhile about what you are doing. Believe me, I have painted some terrible canvases. I still do bad paintings every now and then; just not so frequently anymore.

In retrospect, many of those problem paintings do have some good parts, or are compositionally sound, or are charming in their own weird way. It would be the same for you. Your older, odder work has much to teach you. If you don't have such artwork behind you, then now is the time to start making some, without worrying about it being all that good. That's not the point at this stage. The same goes for embarking on a new body of work, even if you are accomplished at what you do.

If you have ever listened to outtakes, rare recordings, and different studio or live versions of familiar songs, as well as other experimental recordings by musicians that you admire, then you can see the parallel. It is years of practicing, honing skills and developing a musical sensibility, combined with a willingness to TRY SOMETHING DIFFERENT, that makes for the ability to create wonderful songs and other musical compositions. If along the way, some peculiar things are recorded, then who cares? Their fans and yours will always be interested to hear and see the process.

Listening to the recordings I mentioned earlier reminded me that it takes a lot of experimentation, serious play and hard work to get to the finished product from the very first thought; the first glimmer of a spark that eventually becomes a great song.

And so it is. If an artistic impulse comes to you, grab it and see what you can do with it. Take anything from this book; take my raw ideas, add your interpretations, combine a bit of this and delete some of that, and see where you could possibly go with it. If any one thing in this book doesn't do it for you, then there at least 299 other things you can do. And don't forget to have some fun along the way. Make beautiful visual music while drawing out the muses.

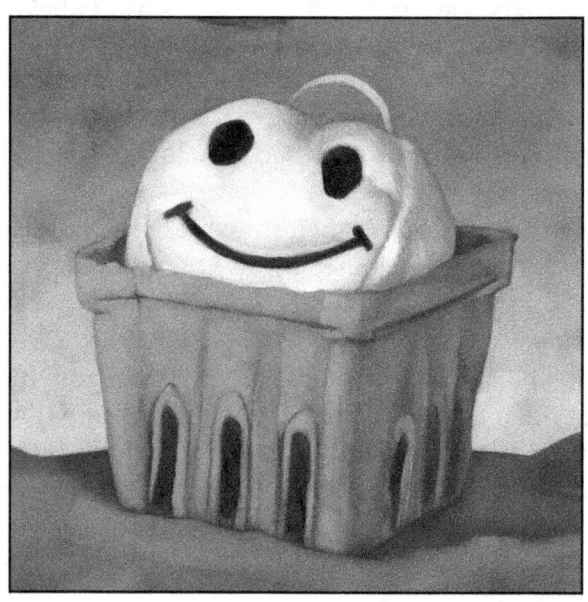

More Books by Alexandria Levin

Pricing Your Artwork with Confidence
An extensive step-by-step guide to pricing artwork and fine craftwork

Coming soon:
Pulling Abstraction from Realism

More titles are being developed for 2015 and beyond
in both print and ebook formats.

Go to www.paintedjay.com for information and updates
on book availability and other news.

Connection Portal

Painted Jay Publishing
www.paintedjay.com

Alexandria Levin – oil paintings
www.alexalev.com

**Alexandria Levin – graphic design, web development,
lyric poetry and accidental photography**
www.alexandrialevin.com

Bright Pink Smile – art blog
www.brightpinksmile.com

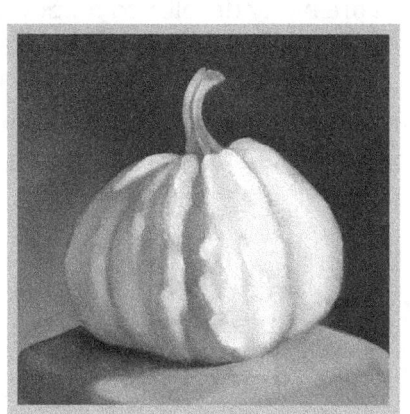

www.ingramcontent.com/pod-product-compliance
Lightning Source LLC
Chambersburg PA
CBHW080909170526
45158CB00008B/2047